NATIONAL LEAGUE OF COTILLIONS™

~

# THE OFFICIAL BOOK OF

# ELECTRONIC ETIQUETTE

CHARLES AND ANNE WINTERS

*DEDICATION*

*This book is dedicated to our children, Elizabeth Anne
and Charles Anthony Winters. We are proud of their example
of treating others with honor, dignity and respect.*

THE OFFICIAL BOOK OF ELECTRONIC ETIQUETTE

ISBN: 0-9710644-1-5
Library of Congress Control Number: 2001090102

*Penmark*
PUBLISHING
P.O. BOX 49428, CHARLOTTE, NC 28277

Printed in the United States of America

# CONTENTS

# &INTRODUCTION

*D*uring the past few years, we have become engulfed in a tidal wave of technology. It has greatly accelerated the speed of communication, given instant access to data and made life more convenient. At the same time, society has been drowning in a sea of information overload and time pressure that often results in rudeness and incivility.

Every year the National League of Cotillions teaches etiquette, social skills and character education to thousands of students of all ages – from pre-kindergarten to adults. In the process, we have learned that courtesy must extend far beyond face-to-face encounters. For example, what you say in a text message or a voice mail reflects your personality as much as a handshake. As you will discover, manners are equally as important as machines.

The topics of this book are presented in a question-answer format.

- When is using a cell phone inappropriate?
- What should I do if it is absolutely necessary to take incoming calls in a public place?
- What limits should be placed on the use of a home computer by family members?
- Are there specific courtesies when using video and digital cameras?

- How can I help keep my cell phone from disturbing my schedule?
- What courtesies apply to Instant Messaging and "buddy lists?"
- What guidelines should be observed when replying to an e-mail message?
- What is the correct way to answer a phone call at home?
- What are the "Seven W's" of taking phone messages?
- What electronic courtesies are expected on airplanes and in restaurants.
- What rules should be established for music in the home?
- What is considered good etiquette for leaving messages on someone's business voice mail?
- Is there a gracious way to shorten a call? And how should it be concluded?
- What are the basic rules to follow when faxing?
- Should children have their own telephones?

You will find answers to these questions, and more.

The final chapter presents a parent-child guide to electronic etiquette – including the use of home computers, phones, music, DVDs, digital games and more. We emphasize the importance of setting boundaries for children at an early age. The principles you establish are building blocks that will shape their character and attitude for a lifetime.

It is our sincere desire that this book will help you, your family and your associates keep the focus on good manners and courtesy in this electronic age.

*– Charles and Anne Winters*

# Chapter One

# Cell Phone Courtesies

Professional golfer John Cook was about to taste victory. He was tied for the lead on the seventeenth hole of the Sony Open at the Waialae Country Club in Honolulu, Hawaii.

Then, on his backswing at the par-three hole, a cell phone began to ring near the tee box. Cook was distracted and the shot ended up in a bunker near the green. Clearly upset, the 10-time winner on the PGA tour grumbled, "Ahhhhh! Whose cell phone?"

Cook bogeyed the hole and lost the tournament to Jerry Kelly by one stroke. Instead of a $720,000 payday, his second-place finish reduced his winnings to $432,000. That was an expensive cell phone call!

Even more disturbing, as one witness recounted, "The thoughtless spectator answered the phone and started talking!"

*The thoughtless spectator answered the phone and started talking!*

For better or worse, the rapid proliferation of wireless phones has revolutionized the way people communicate with each other. They not only keep individuals in constant contact, but also are invaluable in emergencies.

Over half of the people in the United States use cell phones daily. Parents keep in touch with their children and executives talk with their fast-paced associates.

Unfortunately, many users of mobile phones have developed habits that have been described as rude, ill-mannered and discourteous. Some medical doctors are reporting cases of "cell phone rage" that have resulted in black eyes and broken bones.

Today, an increasing number of restaurants have established "cell-free" zones. In Europe, many trains have phone-free sections.

The National League of Cotillions has established the following ways to master productivity and politeness when using your cell phone.

## STAY SAFE

Be alert and use your wireless phone to help others in

*CASES OF "CELL PHONE RAGE" HAVE RESULTED IN BLACK EYES AND BROKEN BONES.*

emergencies. According to the Cellular Telecommunications Industry Association (CTIA), cell phones are used approximately 100,000 times every day in the U.S. to dial 911 and other emergency numbers. They help to save lives and report other dangerous situations.

### *How can one have a safer cell phone experience while driving?*

*THE RISK OF AN AUTOMOBILE ACCIDENT QUADRUPLES WHEN TALKING ON A CELL PHONE.*

*A* Toronto study reported in the *New England Journal of Medicine* found that the risk of an automobile accident *quadruples* when talking on a cell phone. The distraction caused by the device has been named by Harvard University's Center for Risk Analysis as the reason for a half million crashes and over 2,600 highway deaths each year. As a result, many states are considering laws and restrictions regarding mobile phone use. New York was the first state to totally ban cell phone use by drivers.

You show consideration for others when you take responsibility for the manner in which you use a wireless phone while driving.

You will stay much safer and show respect by following these important rules:

*NEVER TAKE NOTES OR LOOK UP PHONE NUMBERS WHILE DRIVING.*

❖ Inform the person you are speaking with that you are driving ( in case you are disconnected).

❖ If you must talk while driving, use voice-activated dialing, an ear piece, and a clip-on or sun visor microphone. Better yet, have a hands-free phone installed in your car by a professional.

❖ Don't try to put your ear piece on while driving.

❖ Make it a habit to find a safe place to stop before dialing (unless you have voice-activated dialing).

❖ Keep your hands on the wheel and your eyes on the road.

❖ Remember that changing lanes and tapping a cell phone keypad are not compatible.

❖ Know your phone well enough to activate it quickly.

❖ Use speed dialing (or one-touch redial) whenever possible.

❖ Never take notes or look up phone numbers while driving.

❖ Suspend calls in heavy traffic or during hazardous weather.

❖ Avoid stressful phone conversations while driving.

❖ Never use your phone in congested traffic areas.

If you find it necessary to use your phone while driving, make it a habit to get in your car, buckle up and prepare your voice-activated phone, ear piece or hands-free device before starting your engine.

Better yet, follow the advice of a bumper sticker distributed by a radio station: "Drive Now, Talk Later."

**In addition to driving, are there additional safety issues involved with cell phones?**

*N*ever attempt to use a cell phone while on an airplane since it can cause interference with sensitive radio transmission. The exception, of course, is if there is a situation that needs to be reported to officials. Also avoid using your phone in hospitals – especially near an emergency room or surgery area. It may affect patient monitoring devices and even heart pacemakers.

## SHOW RESPECT

**Is it impolite to use your cell phone in the company of associates or friends?**

*W*hen you take a call in the presence of a special client or personal friend, you are communicating, "You are secondary

*MAKE IT A HABIT TO GET INTO YOUR CAR, BUCKLE UP AND PREPARE YOUR VOICE-ACTIVATED PHONE, EAR PIECE OR HANDS-FREE DEVICE BEFORE STARTING YOUR ENGINE.*

– the caller is more important than you."

If you are expecting an important call, let the person know in advance, and excuse yourself before taking the call, which should be kept very brief. If the conversation requires longer than one minute, arrange for a more convenient time to complete the call. Also:

*Do Not Receive a Call When Someone Has an Appointment With You – or When You Have Guests. It's Rude!*

❖ Avoid calling someone on his or her cell phone without prior permission. Remember, that person is paying for incoming calls.

❖ Do not receive a call when someone has an appointment with you – or when you have guests. It's rude!

❖ Remember to charge your batteries. It is not polite for a conversation to be interrupted due to low power.

❖ Never use a cell phone on a date. It shows disrespect to your companion. Turn off the phone unless you are expecting an emergency call.

❖ Don't ignore the waitperson in a restaurant or a retail clerk because you are using your cell phone. You are infringing on that person's valuable time.

❖ If you are on a speaker phone, always inform the person you are talking with. It respects the person's privacy.

Parents, if your children are involved in sporting events,

give them your full attention. This is not a time to conduct business or chat with friends. Give your children the respect they deserve.

And one more word of caution. Don't be the person who talks in a noisy room with his finger in one ear – then reaches out to shake hands with an associate! It is unhygienic.

# HONOR PRIVACY

***Why don't people understand that I would prefer not to overhear their cell phone talk?***

People are often embarrassed when they hear one-sided conversations regarding health issues, family problems or business deals.

Honor people's privacy:

❖ Never call during meal times, early morning or late at night.
❖ Do not make important business decisions from a cell phone in a public place.
❖ Golf courses and sporting events are places to get away from business. Turn off your phone.
❖ Always assume that someone may eavesdrop on your conversation.

*THE WORDS YOU SPEAK ARE FAR MORE IMPORTANT THAN THE TECHNOLOGY THAT TRANSMITS THEM.*

*– YVETTE SHALCROSS, COTILLION DIRECTOR, RALEIGH, NC*

In a public restroom, a gentleman dialed a cell phone number and, in a loud voice, asked, "Hi, how you doing?" The person in the next stall responded, "Just fine, thank you!"

# SPEAK QUIETLY

### *Why do people tend to speak so loudly while using a cell phone?*

*M*any individuals fail to realize that a mobile phone is a high-tech instrument that will operate properly even if you speak in a lower than normal voice tone.

❖ Don't yell! Let the phone do the work.
❖ Turn your incoming audio volume to maximum. When you hear well, you will speak softer.
❖ Learn to use text messaging (discussed later in this chapter and in Chapter Three).
❖ Never call attention to yourself – by a loud ring, or a loud voice.
❖ If you are required to use your cell phone for a conference call, speak from a quiet location – never from a noisy atmosphere. You'll end up talking too loud.
❖ Do not use your phone while eating a meal. Can you imagine what you sound like talking and chewing food at the same time – even with a hands-free microphone?

*NEVER CALL ATTENTION TO YOURSELF – BY A LOUD RING, OR A LOUD VOICE.*

❖ Never allow people close by to overhear your conversation.

# DON'T DISTURB

*R*ecently, during a Broadway performance, an actor stopped the show when a cell phone rang and the patron began speaking. He asked the person to leave the theater – and there was a standing ovation.

### When is using a cell phone inappropriate?

*I*n social and business situations, remember to turn off your phone. There is no rule that says you must constantly be "on call." Ask yourself, "Will my conversation disturb others?"

Never place or receive a call, or allow the phone to ring or beep, during a meal, meeting, religious service, wedding or funeral. Be sure to turn your phone off, or switch to "vibrate," when in the theater, doctor's office, elevator, museum, library or public restroom.

Some business firms are now asking clients to check their cell phones at the reception desk. And many school districts have rules that ban cell phones from the classroom. (They must be kept in lockers.) If parents need to reach their child at school, they should call the principal's office. Always be

*IN SOCIAL AND BUSINESS SITUATIONS, REMEMBER TO TURN OFF YOUR PHONE. THERE IS NO RULE THAT SAYS YOU MUST CONSTANTLY BE "ON CALL."*

aware of your current school cell phone policy and respect that decision.

Most court rooms require that all cell phones be turned off.

❖ Explain in advance if you must answer your phone while in a social or business situation. Ask the caller to hold, then excuse yourself and exit the room before continuing the call.

❖ Use the "vibrate" feature whenever possible.

❖ If phone is set on "ring," try to answer at the first sound.

❖ Set the ring tone at its lowest level.

Willie Brown, the mayor of San Francisco, said, "The single most offensive thing you can do is come to a meeting with your cell phone on." A person witnessed a seminar participant actually crawl under a table to answer a call.

One organization set this rule: "The person whose cell phone goes off first buys lunch for the group!" People got the message.

*EXPLAIN IN ADVANCE IF YOU MUST ANSWER YOUR PHONE WHILE IN A SOCIAL OR BUSINESS SITUATION.*

# AIM FOR SILENCE

**It is difficult to find peace and quiet when wireless phone users are nearby.**

I'm sure you have heard a cell phone ring and have seen

three or four people reach for their phones. The sound of the incoming call and the noise of the conversation can be annoying. That is why mobile units are being banned in so many places.

Take every precaution to make sure your phone is not aggravating others.

❖ When people are present, use silent or vibrating options – or press "Power off."

❖ Caller ID allows you to see the caller's name and number before deciding whether you should excuse yourself and take the call.

❖ Become fully acquainted with the call forwarding and voice mail features of your phone.

❖ Screen every call and only answer in an emergency when in the presence of others.

❖ If you don't plan to take calls, turn the unit off. It is distracting to let the phone ring and ring and ring.

Some professionals – such as medical doctors – must have their cell phones or beepers on at all times. They should use the silent options and seek privacy to take calls.

*THE BATHTUB WAS INVENTED IN 1850, THE TELEPHONE IN 1875. IF YOU HAD LIVED IN 1850, YOU COULD HAVE SAT IN THE BATHTUB FOR 25 YEARS WITHOUT HEARING THE PHONE RING!*

*– JACOB M. BRADUE*

# KEEP YOUR DISTANCE

*How far should I move away from people before making a call?*

Good manners require that you move to a location where others cannot hear your conversation. That is usually at least ten to fifteen feet away. Better yet, find a space that is totally private. If that is not possible, wait to make or take calls.

Also, when standing in an ATM line, back away from the person in front of you before using your phone.

# GIVE AN EXPLANATION

*What should I do if it is absolutely necessary to take incoming calls in a public place?*

If you must keep your phone on, explain the reason to those around you. Say, "I am expecting an important call. I hope you will understand."

❖ If at a conference or a restaurant, sit near an exit.
❖ Place your phone on vibrator mode.
❖ Leave the room to take the call.

*GOOD MANNERS REQUIRE THAT YOU MOVE TO A LOCATION WHERE OTHERS CANNOT HEAR YOUR CONVERSATION. THAT IS USUALLY TEN TO FIFTEEN FEET AWAY.*

# MANAGE YOUR TIME

### *How can I help keep my cell phone from disturbing my schedule?*

ar too many people allow incoming calls to take precedent over almost every activity. It decreases their productivity and constantly disrupts their day. Here's how to avoid such problems.

> ❖ Whenever possible, use voice mail for incoming calls and return them at a convenient place and time.
>
> ❖ Keep your call time short.
>
> ❖ To decrease the number of incoming calls, do not give your cell phone number out too freely.
>
> ❖ In your office, take calls at your desk, not while walking up and down the halls.
>
> ❖ Always let the other party know you are calling from a cell phone, in case the service is disrupted.
>
> ❖ Set aside specific, scheduled times to return calls on your voice mail.

Remember, you will be more productive by knowing the features of your phone. Practice the art of emergency use. Learn how to quickly access silent modes, voice mail, and more.

*ALWAYS LET THE OTHER PARTY KNOW YOU ARE CALLING FROM A CELL PHONE, IN CASE THE SERVICE IS DISRUPTED.*

# DON'T BE A SHOW-OFF

### *Why do some people use their cell phones to look and act important?*

*I*t's sad but true that some individuals actually ask people to call them – so they will look important. I'm sure you have seen those who have two or more electronic devices strapped to their belt. Hopefully, they have a good reason.

> ❖ Never use a cell phone to impress others.
> ❖ Don't try to dazzle people with your multi-tasking abilities.
> ❖ Don't wear your earpiece when not on the phone.
> ❖ Never place your cell phone on a restaurant table.
> ❖ Your phone is not a status symbol. It is merely a tool for communicating!

Also, unless you are a child, don't use novelty rings. No one likes to hear "Mary Had a Little Lamb" or "The Minute Waltz" blaring from your phone!

*YOUR PHONE IS NOT A STATUS SYMBOL. IT IS MERELY A TOOL FOR COMMUNICATING.*

# TEXT TELEPHONES

*E*very minute of every hour, millions of messages are being exchanged between wireless phones – not voice memos, but typed words that appear on tiny screens. "B HOME 7:30."

Or, "CU TOMORROW."

The concept is not new. Text telephones were invented in the 1930s and were popular with journalists who could feed their stories directly to newspaper editors. Then, in the 1960s, Robert Weitbrecht, a deaf scientist, created a teletypewriter that allowed the hearing-impaired to communicate on existing telephone networks.

Today, instead of bulky units, we type on little handheld keyboards and retrieve messages on our beepers or wireless phones. Current script designers added the feature more as a novelty rather than a serious option. Now it has become an essential part of communication.

Text telephones (first in Europe and Asia, then the U.S.) began with personal use, but many in business and government find them extremely valuable. For example, airlines use them to relay flight information to gate agents.

Why has the short message service (SMS) text system become so popular?

❖ It's inexpensive, using less airtime than a voice call.

❖ It's convenient – forget about busy signals.

❖ It's discreet – you can send and receive messages at times when it is not appropriate to talk. For example: at sports events, on public transportation and at restaurants.

Some services deliver news, stock quotes and sports scores

*TEXT TELEPHONES WERE INVENTED IN THE 1930S AND LATER BECAME USEFUL FOR THE HEARING-IMPAIRED.*

at the customer's request.

### What abbreviations are acceptable when sending text messages?

*B*ecause the message being sent and received is limited (usually 160 units including spaces), people have become quite original in creating shortcuts.

In Chapter Three you will find symbols and abbreviations used in e-mail, but text messaging is creating a language all its own.

Since a single button on a cell phone numeric keypad has three or four letters, you may have to press more than once to enter the letter you need. It only makes sense to press as few strokes as possible – that's why abbreviations seem so necessary.

Here are just a few examples of how people shorten their words and sentences:

| | |
|---|---|
| ATB | – All the best. |
| B | – Be. |
| BTW | – By the way. |
| ENUF | – Enough. |
| IN or N | – Replaces "ing" word endings. For example: CALLN or DOIN. |
| IM | – I am. |

*W*ITH TEXT MESSAGES... YOU CAN SAY THINGS YOU WOULDN'T BE ABLE TO SAY FACE TO FACE.

*-- DR. GUY FIELDING*

| IMS | – I am sorry. |
| INO | – I know. |
| J4F | – Just for fun. |
| MI | – May I? |
| MIP | – May I please? |
| NE1 | – Anyone. |
| NOM | – No, Ma'am. |
| NS | – No, Sir. |
| PC | – Please call. |
| PME | – Pardon me. |
| R | – Are. |
| XLNT | – Excellent. |
| YM | – Yes, Ma'am. |
| YR | – Your. |
| YS | – Yes, Sir. |

In many cases, numbers replace words. For example, the number "2" replaces "to" or "too." You may enter 2DAY instead of "today." And 2G4U is used for "too good for you."

The number "8" is used when a syllable sounds like "ate." L8ER means "later." GR8 means "great." W84ME is used for "wait for me."

When two people use mobile messaging to communicate with each other over long periods of time, their keystrokes become shorter and shorter – yet the communication remains clear.

*EFFICIENT ELECTRONIC LINGO IS SHOWING UP IN...NOTES PASSED IN CLASS, SNAIL MAIL CORRESPONDENCE, EVEN THE ESTEEMED OXFORD DICTIONARY.*

*– PHILADELPHIA ENQUIRER*

# THE NATIONAL LEAGUE OF COTILLIONS
## OFFICIAL RULES OF
## CELL PHONE ETIQUETTE

1. ***Stay safe.*** Before starting your engine, prepare your hand-free devices (voice-activated dialing, ear pieces and clip-on microphones) to be used while driving. Better yet, park your car before making or taking calls.

2. ***Show respect.*** Those you are with should always take precedence over a call.

3. ***Honor privacy.*** Never place calls during meal times, early morning or late at night.

4. ***Speak quietly.*** Keep your voice volume low.

5. ***Don't disturb.*** Never place or receive calls during a meal or meeting, or in a church, theater, court room or public event.

6. ***Aim for silence.*** When others are present, use silent or vibrating options, or turn off the phone.

7. ***Keep your distance.*** Move to a location where others cannot hear your conversation.

8. ***Give an explanation.*** If you must keep your phone on, explain the reason to those around you.

9. ***Manage your time.*** Whenever possible, use voice mail for incoming calls and return them at a convenient place and time.

10. ***Don't be a show-off.*** Never use a cell phone to impress others.

# CHAPTER TWO

# PHONES AND DIGITAL MANNERS AT HOME

We have come a long way from March 10, 1876, when Alexander Graham Bell, the inventor of the telephone, made the first call to his assistant, Thomas Watson, who was in a nearby room. "Mr. Watson," he said, "come here. I want to see you."

That was the start of a revolution in communications that has linked our world together in unforseen ways. However, the effective use of today's technology still depends on people who treat others with honor, dignity and respect.

*THE REVOLUTION IN COMMUNICATIONS HAS LINKED OUR WORLD TOGETHER IN UNFORSEEN WAYS.*

## PHONE ETIQUETTE

The telephone is a vital communication tool. We use it every day to keep in touch with friends and relatives, make dinner or theater reservations, conduct banking and other business, and even register for college courses. And in times of emergency, the telephone is absolutely essential. But despite its many wonderful uses, the telephone can become a source of contention in your home.

Let's face it, we have all become irritated at times by:

❖ The sound of someone dialing while you are talking.

❖ A telemarketer who interrupts the family dinner.

❖ A family member who stays on the phone too long.

❖ Trying to locate a misplaced cordless phone.

Don't despair! It is possible to have a phone-friendly home where communication hassles are kept to a minimum. The key is to have clear guidelines that are established by the head of the household and followed by every family member – including the children.

The four basic telephone rules, which we will discuss in this chapter, are:

1. *Set the hours and situations when you should and should not make or receive calls.*
2. *Determine the maximum length of time for calls.*
3. *Establish a specific style of answering and placing calls.*
4. *Have an official message-taking system.*

*YOUR SCHEDULE SHOULD BE GOVERNED BY YOU, NOT BY THE RINGING OF A PHONE.*

*– CATHERINE COREY, COTILLION DIRECTOR, KANSAS CITY, KS*

When reasonable rules and boundaries are understood and practiced, you'll find the phone becomes a friend – instead of a foe – in your home.

# PLUGGING IN

*J*ust because the builder wired every room in your house with a phone jack, doesn't mean you are required to install a dozen units. As you will see, there are locations where you should, and *should not*, have a phone.

**Specifically, where should telephones be placed in the home?**

*P*erhaps you have visited someone who has a phone in every room – and when they all ring it sounds like a telethon or a switchboard center. The key here is to keep it simple. You don't need any more phones than are necessary.

Here is where they should be located:

- ❖ Telephones, either cordless or permanent, should be placed in the kitchen, master bedroom, home office and guest bedroom.
- ❖ Install a phone close to (but not in) the family room, since calls might interfere with those engaged in conversation or other activities.

*WHEN REASONABLE RULES AND BOUNDARIES ARE UNDERSTOOD AND PRACTICED, YOU'LL FIND THE PHONE BECOMES A FRIEND – INSTEAD OF A FOE.*

❖ Be sure the location is convenient and in a well-lighted place for taking messages.

### What locations should be avoided when placing phones?

*D*o *not* have a phone in either the dining room or recreation room. Those areas are for other purposes.

We do not recommend having telephones in the bedrooms of children in your home. We will discuss the reason in Chapter Seven.

*H*ONOR THE PRIVACY OF INDIVIDUALS UNLESS THEY ASKED TO BE CALLED DURING SPECIFIC HOURS.

## PHONE TIMES

### What time should calls be made – and what hours should be avoided?

*W*hen dialing someone's home, be on the safe side and don't call before 9:00 A.M. or after 9:00 P.M. Also do not place calls during meal times. Honor the privacy of individuals unless they ask to be called during specific hours.

The exceptions to the recommended phone hours are (1) when prior arrangements have been made, and (2) when it is an emergency.

Always be aware of the time zone you are calling. Don't

disregard the three-hour difference between Los Angeles and New York.

### Should I answer the phone every time it rings?

*A* couple in Detroit was having a Sunday afternoon visit in the home of friends, when the phone rang. "Aren't you going to answer that?" the visiting husband asked. "No," the host replied. "Your company is much more important."

If the call is urgent, the person can leave a message on the answering machine.

You are in control of the phone – the phone is not in control of you! Always ask yourself this question: What is more important, my current activity or this interruption? Who takes precedent, the person I am with or the unknown person who is calling?

Also, don't answer the phone at meal times (and make sure the friends of your children know you do not take calls when the family is dining together). Let the call be received by voice mail or your answering machine.

Other times when you, or members of your family, should choose not to answer the phone include:

❖ Family time.
❖ When children are involved in homework or music practice.
❖ Quiet times when you are reading, reflecting, or even taking a nap.

*YOU ARE IN CONTROL OF THE PHONE – THE PHONE IS NOT IN CONTROL OF YOU!*

# WATCH THE CLOCK

*B*oth incoming and outgoing calls should be kept to a fifteen minute maximum – and much shorter when possible. Exceptions include when you are dealing with health issues, important personal matters, or having a conversation with an elderly person who may be lonely.

# ANSWERING THE PHONE

*We* believe the adage: "You never have a second chance to make a first impression." That is why the first words you say when picking up the receiver are so vital.

When the phone rings you may have no idea who has dialed, yet you need to answer with the same courtesy as if you knew the incoming call was from your best friend.

Receiving a call should be viewed as greeting someone in person. Focus on the individual and communicate joy and enthusiasm. It should always be a pleasure for the caller to hear your voice. Even though you may be in the middle of a major project, give the caller the impression that you are happy the phone rang. If you can't answer with a positive attitude,

let the call go to voice mail or an answering machine.

After answering the phone properly, you might say, "Donna, how are you? I haven't heard from you in so long." Instead of just, "How's it going?"

You honor and respect others when you let them know how important they are – whether the call is for you, or for another person.

## What is the correct way to answer a phone call at home?

The ideal time to pick up the phone is between the third and fourth rings. Don't race to the phone, or you will sound as if you are out of breath. Also, answering on the first ring may rush – or even startle – the caller.

IMPROPER: "Hello?" – and nothing more.

PROPER: "Hello, this is Mary Jones." Or, "Jones residence. This is Mary Jones speaking."

NOTE: When you are the guest in someone's home or you have been *requested* to answer the phone, ask how it should be answered. The recommended response is: "Taylor residence. Bill James speaking."

## How should I respond if the call is for another person?

Regardless of who the call is for, you should always answer in a calm, courteous manner. Don't be like some who

*IF YOU CAN'T ANSWER WITH A POSITIVE ATTITUDE, LET THE CALL GO TO VOICE MAIL OR AN ANSWERING MACHINE.*

give the impression you have imposed on their time and interrupted something important.

Follow these guidelines:

❖ If the caller does not identify himself or herself, it is proper to ask, "May I say who is calling?" (If you know the individual, greet the person warmly before continuing.)
❖ Continue, "Just a moment, please."
❖ Place the receiver down quietly and move away before requesting a specific person to come to the phone. Never yell out an individual's name.

### What if the person being called is not at home?

*F*or safety reasons, never indicate whether the person is physically present or not. Say, "(Name) is not available to come to the phone right now. May I please take a message?"

See: TAKING AND LEAVING MESSAGES later in this chapter.

### What if someone other than you answers the phone and it is an individual you do not wish to speak with?

*N*ever ask family members to be dishonest by saying, "He's not here." Instead, they should say, "I'm sorry, he is

*FOR SAFETY REASONS, NEVER INDICATE WHETHER THE PERSON IS PHYSICALLY PRESENT OR NOT.*

unavailable right now. He will have to call you back later. May I take a message?"

Have a family discussion regarding the ethics and integrity of answering the phone. This issue is important to character building and to the reputation of your family.

### *How should a housekeeper answer the phone?*

*A*n individual working at your home should answer, "Williams residence. Mary Jones speaking." Also, instruct a housekeeper regarding how to take a proper message (as discussed later in this chapter).

## PLACING A CALL

### *What preparation should I make before placing a call?*

*F*irst, make sure you have the correct number. If you don't have it memorized, write it down. Next, determine the purpose of the call. Other than a social conversation with a close friend, you should never place a call without a reason or objective. Before dialing the number, make a note of the topics you want to cover. If it is a long distance call, pay attention to the time zone differences.

If no one answers and there is no answering machine, allow the phone to ring approximately seven times before hanging up. It is annoying for a phone to ring and the caller be

*Have a family discussion regarding the ethics and integrity of answering the phone.*

too impatient to allow the person to reach the phone. If you reach an answering machine, leave a proper message; don't just hang up.

Unless the conversation is purely social, treat every call as a mini-meeting by setting an agenda and deciding what action needs to be taken.

### What should be my first words?

*M*AKE A
HABIT OF
ASKING, "IS
THIS A GOOD
TIME TO
TALK?"

Identify yourself immediately. Say "Hello. This is Bill Johnson." Don't expect people to recognize your voice. Never tease, "Guess who this is!"

Ask for the person you wish to speak with: "May I please speak to Martha Smith?" Always use first and last names unless you are a personal friend. Never say, "Can I speak with ...."

IMPROPER: "Is Martha there?" The person who answers the phone may have to ask, "Martha who?"

PROPER: "Hello. This is Bill Johnson. May I please speak with Martha Smith?"

- ❖ When you have reached the desired party, identify yourself, greet the person warmly and state the purpose of your call.
- ❖ Never say: "What are you doing?" or "What's happening over there?"
- ❖ Make a habit of asking, "Is this a good time to

talk?" If it is not, ask, "When would be a convenient time to call back?"

NOTE: If you know the person who answers the phone, greet that individual warmly before being transferred to the desired party. If you call a number frequently and the same person answers the phone, take the time to engage in a brief, friendly conversation.

### What if I reach a wrong number?

*G*et in the habit of dialing slowly and carefully to reach the right party. If you don't have the number memorized, be sure it is written down clearly.

If you dial incorrectly and an unexpected voice comes on the line, don't panic! Ask, "Is this 704-867-3167?" If it is not, apologize and say, "I'm sorry. I must have the wrong number." Then end the call. Never slam down the phone.

### Should I place a call from another person's phone?

*N*ever make any calls from the phone of your host or hostess without their prior permission. Don't charge long distance calls, even *with* their permission. People will be polite, even if they resent the charges. Use a credit card or have it billed to your phone number. Also, since dialing an operator for information can be costly, charge those inquiries to your personal billing. Your host should have a directory

*NEVER MAKE ANY CALLS FROM THE PHONE OF YOUR HOST OR HOSTESS WITHOUT THEIR PRIOR PERMISSION.*

near every phone. If not, ask for one politely.

### *How can I help make the call a positive experience?*

*G*ive your total attention to the person you have called. Avoid speaking with others in the room and never attempt to multi-task or work on another project while you are on the phone.

Practice these rules:

❖ Refrain from eating or drinking while you are talking. Although the person cannot see you, he can *hear* you.
❖ Attempt to mentally picture the person you are conversing with. It helps give more life to the conversation.
❖ Show continuing interest in the conversation by saying, "Yes" or "I see."
❖ Respond to long answers with an "I agree" or "I'm sorry" along the way.
❖ If you are disconnected, the person placing the call (the host or hostess) phones back.

## ENDING THE CALL

### *Is there a gracious way to shorten a call? And how should it be concluded?*

*IF YOU ARE DISCONNECTED, THE PERSON PLACING THE CALL (THE HOST OR HOSTESS) PHONES BACK.*

$\mathscr{S}$ince you placed the call, it is your responsibility to end the conversation. However, the person you are speaking with may have the "gift of gab" or be an individual who doesn't watch the clock. Here's how you can politely bring the conversation to a conclusion:

❖ Use phrases such as:
  "Before I must go, let me tell you....."
  "I know you are busy so I'll let you go."
  "Thanks for your time."
  "Please forgive me, but I have a busy schedule today."
❖ End the call with something positive, such as:
  "It's always good to talk with you." " Thanks for calling." "It's been fun chatting."
❖ Replace the receiver gently.

The question often arises, "How do I end the call if I have not *made* the call?"

If you know the person is long-winded, state at the start of the conversation, "I am so glad you called, but I only have a few minutes."

To end the call, take control. Say something such as, "I just looked at my watch and realize we will have to continue this conversation later."

*$\mathscr{E}$ND THE CALL WITH SOMETHING POSITIVE, SUCH AS, "IT'S ALWAYS GOOD TO TALK WITH YOU."*

# YOUR PHONE VOICE

*A* phone conversation may be hidden from view, but you are making a lasting impression. The sound of your voice is extremely important.

Studies have shown that when a person is smiling as he or she speaks, that same warmth comes through the phone. One young man actually placed a mirror beside his telephone so he could *see* himself smile. "It truly changed my attitude on the phone," he exclaimed.

Here are ways to improve the way you sound.

*ADD ENERGY AND EXCITEMENT TO YOUR VOICE.*

❖ Keep the telephone at least one inch from your mouth so that you will not sound garbled.

❖ Make sure your volume is neither too loud nor too soft.

❖ Speak at a rate slightly slower than normal for greater clarity.

❖ Vary your tone and pitch to add vocal variety.

❖ Deliberately add energy and excitement to your voice.

One of our cotillion directors told us, "Some callers lift your soul, and others leave you depressed. Some people you look forward to talking with, and some you don't."

What are *you* communicating to others through your voice

and conversation? Perhaps it's time to record a phone call and give yourself an honest self-evaluation.

# PROBLEMS TO AVOID

*P*erhaps you have tried to speak when the radio or television is blaring in the background. Turn down the volume!

Try to eliminate *all* background noise – whether from people, audio, or poor phone technology. Always apologize to the caller for any extraneous sounds coming through the phone.

Also, keep in mind:

- ❖ Should you need to sneeze or cough, quickly turn your head and cover both your mouth and the phone receiver.
- ❖ Some phones are equipped with a "mute" button. Learn how to quickly locate this feature and use as needed.
- ❖ Don't cradle the phone in your neck. It not only distorts your voice, but can eventually cause personal physical damage.
- ❖ If you must put the receiver down, do so gently.

# TAKING AND LEAVING MESSAGES

*A* great way to keep track of telephone messages is to

*TRY TO ELIMINATE ALL BACKGROUND NOISE – WHETHER FROM PEOPLE, AUDIO, OR POOR PHONE TECHNOLOGY.*

establish an official family "message center" near the phone in your kitchen. All written phone messages should be posted there, with a space for each member of the household.

Please use either THE OFFICIAL MESSAGE PAD™ , note paper or a Post-it™ pad at every phone in your home. Notes should be taken to the message center immediately.

It is helpful to have a telephone directory near every phone. Otherwise you may be absorbing large charges to obtain numbers from an information operator. Call your phone service provider for extra books.

The message center should include emergency numbers for police, fire, poison control center, doctors and phone numbers for parents at work.

*ESTABLISH AN OFFICIAL FAMILY "MESSAGE CENTER" NEAR THE PHONE IN YOUR KITCHEN.*

### What information is necessary when writing telephone messages?

*U*se the "Seven W's" when writing a phone memo:

1. *Who* is the message for?
2. *When* was the message received? (Date and time)
3. *Who* is the message from?
4. *What* is the message?
5. *Where* should the call be returned? (Phone number)
6. *When* is the best time to return the call? (Date and time)
7. *Who* took the message?

## THE OFFICIAL MESSAGE PAD™
### THE 7 W'S

FOR: _____
1. WHO IS THE MESSAGE FOR?

DATE: _____ TIME: _____
2. WHEN WAS THE MESSAGE RECEIVED?

FROM: _____
3. WHO IS THE MESSAGE FROM?

MESSAGE: _____
4. WHAT IS THIS MESSAGE?

_____

_____

_____

PHONE: _____
5. WHERE SHOULD THE CALL BE RETURNED?

CALL (TIME): _____
6. WHEN IS THE BEST TIME TO RETURN THE CALL?

SIGNED: _____
7. WHO RECEIVED THE MESSAGE?

© PENMARK PUBLISHING / NATIONAL LEAGUE OF COTILLIONS www.nljc.com

Order information for THE OFFICIAL MESSAGE PAD™
(self-stick) may be found at www.nljc.com.

*B*e sure you give the caller your full attention. Write

*B*E SURE TO
*GIVE THE*
*CALLER YOUR*
*FULL*
*ATTENTION.*

clearly and deliver the message without delay.

Never reply with impatience when you are asked to take a message. Sound as if you are delighted with the task. Follow the Golden Rule: If you expect clear, complete messages to be delivered to you, that's how you should prepare them for others.

IMPROPER MESSAGE: Jane called.

PROPER MESSAGE: (1) Mark received a call (2) 4/6 at 6:15 P.M. (3) from Jane Williams. (4) Can get concert tickets for Friday night. Need to know this evening. (5) Call 704-867-3167 (6) before 10 P.M. (7) – Mary (person taking call).

### What guidelines should I follow when leaving a message?

*A*sk, "Do you have a pen and paper handy?" Then give your first and last name and phone number slowly. Don't hesitate to ask the person to repeat the number.

Do not leave private or personal messages with another person.

### Should an R.s.v.p. be answered by telephone?

*A*n invitation to a social event may only be responded to by telephone if a phone number is printed next to the R.s.v.p.

*If you Expect Clear, Complete Messages to be Delivered to You, That's How You Should Prepare Them For Others.*

Otherwise, you should send a written reply. Be sure to reply promptly.

If you are calling to respond to an invitation, repeat the name of the event, place, date and time. This is necessary because:

1. The host or hostess needs to know how many guests to plan for.
2. The person extending the invitation needs to be sure the guest knows the location, time and date of the event.

### Is it permissible to leave a response to an R.s.v.p. on an answering machine?

*Y*ou should attempt (at least twice) to speak personally to the person extending the invitation. If unavailable, leave your response on the machine.

ACCEPTING:
> IMPROPER RESPONSE: "This is Mary. See you at the picnic!"
>
> PROPER RESPONSE: "Hello. This is Mary. I am calling to respond to the invitation to attend the picnic on April 16th from 6 to 9 P.M. at the Regent Club. Bill and I are looking forward to being with you."

*IF YOU ARE CALLING TO RESPOND TO AN INVITATION, REPEAT THE NAME OF THE EVENT, PLACE, DATE AND TIME.*

*YOU SHOULD SET YOUR ANSWERING MACHINE TO RING AT LEAST FIVE TO SEVEN TIMES BEFORE PLAYING YOUR GREETING.*

REGRETTING:

> IMPROPER RESPONSE: "This is Mary. Got your invitation. Sorry we can't make it."

> PROPER RESPONSE: "This is (your name). I am calling to thank you for the invitation to the picnic on April 16th. Unfortunately, we will be unable to attend." If you know the person well, you may give the reason for declining the invitation.

# ANSWERING MACHINES

*V*oice mail and electronic answering devices are both a boon and a bane. Owners of such equipment say, "It makes my life so much easier." Callers, however, aren't so sure.

The majority of homes have a phone equipped with an answering device to play a pre-recorded personal message when you are unavailable.

NOTE: You should set your answering machine to ring at least five to seven times before playing your greeting. This will give you adequate time to reach the phone.

### How can I record the most effective greeting?

*W*e have all listened to greetings that sounded like they were recorded in an echo chamber. Others either shout or speak so softly we can't understand a word.

Always write out your message and practice reading it aloud prior to recording. Here is a recommended greeting for a phone that is used by all members of the family: "Hello. This is the Smith residence. We are unable to answer the phone at this time. Please leave your name and number at the tone and we will return the call as soon as possible."

Avoid saying, "You have reached 704-867-3167," since the caller may have already forgotten your number. Some people are hesitant to give their name, however, callers need to know they have reached the correct residence.

Never use the pre-recorded message that came with your answering machine. Make it personal. Otherwise, the caller may think they have reached the wrong number.

To make your messages more effective, follow these rules:

❖ Wait at least one second after the beeps before your greeting starts.

❖ Move close to the built-in microphone and speak in a normal tone.

❖ Be upbeat! Add some enthusiasm to your voice.

❖ Avoid using music in the background. On a tiny receiver it rarely sounds clear and merely interferes with your message.

❖ Play back your outgoing message. Is it precisely how you want to sound? Do you sound too hurried? Too lifeless and monotonous?

❖ Re-record your greeting until you are satisfied.

*NEVER USE THE PRE-RECORDED MESSAGE THAT CAME WITH YOUR ANSWERING MACHINE. MAKE IT PERSONAL.*

*UNLESS YOUR PROFESSION IS A COMEDIAN AND YOU CHANGE YOUR MESSAGE EVERY DAY, AVOID JOKES, HUMOR AND SATIRE ON YOUR ANSWERING MACHINE.*

How you answer the phone on your machine is just as important as how you would answer in person. You are making a lasting impression.

NOTE: For security reasons, never share your travel plans on an outgoing message. "We'll be on vacation until next Tuesday," is not a smart message to leave.

### Should I use humor on my recorded message?

Perhaps you have dialed a number and heard something like this: "Hi, I'm probably home. I'm just avoiding someone I don't like. Leave me a message and if I don't call back, it's you!"

Unless your profession is a comedian and you change your message every day, avoid jokes, humor and satire on your answering machine. It quickly bores the person who hears it more than once and rarely enhances your image.

NOTE: Don't use a young child to record your greeting. It is unprofessional and is rarely appreciated by those outside your family.

### What rules should I follow when leaving a message?

Some people like to leave a cryptic message such as "It's Bill. Give me a call." The caller assumes you know only one

"Bill," and that you know his number. In reality, you may be miles from your phone directory and don't know how to call the person back.

Follow these guidelines:

- ❖ Keep your message short. Many people set their answering machine to record a maximum of 45 to 60 seconds per message.
- ❖ Speak clearly and slowly when leaving your message, so people will not need to replay it.
- ❖ Avoid leaving jokes or saying, "Guess who this is!" Humor is rarely appreciated in phone messages.
- ❖ Never say "This is urgent" unless it truly is.
- ❖ Leave information concerning only one topic per call. If you have another issue, phone again.
- ❖ Let people know the best time to call you back.
- ❖ Always repeat your name and number twice.
- ❖ Conclude with courtesy – "Thanks," or "Thank you."

IMPROPER: "Hi. This is Judy. Call me about the luncheon."

PROPER: "Hello. This is Judy Smith. I'm calling Sally Jones to remind her about the luncheon at the Hilton at noon on Saturday, May 25th. Please return my call at 890-098-7890. Again, this is Judy Smith at 890-098-7890."

*NEVER SAY "THIS IS URGENT," UNLESS IT TRULY IS.*

### How can I keep up with the large number of incoming messages?

*D*on't allow your messages to pile up. Check your phone several times each day – even if that means access from a remote location.

❖ Keep a pad and paper handy to note phone numbers and any action you must take.

❖ Delete answering machine messages immediately.

❖ Only save a message that contains details someone else needs to hear.

NOTE: Set your phone to ring at least five to seven times to give you a chance to answer the phone (if you choose to).

# VOICE MAIL

*I*f you need an answering system with far more options than answering machines, subscribe to voice mail. It will greatly expand your ability to manage incoming and outgoing messages.

Many homes utilize a multi-box voice mail system, one for each member of the family. Unfortunately, some people use the system as their first line of communication. Don't fall into that trap. Remember, everyone would rather speak person to person.

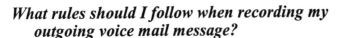
### What rules should I follow when recording my outgoing voice mail message?

*Y*our first objective should be to let people know they have reached the correct number. That's why you should use your own voice for the greeting and identify yourself. Callers don't want to hear a mechanical voice say, "You have reached my voice mail. Please leave your message after the beep."

Follow these rules when recording your message:

❖ To add interest and variety, change your greetings frequently.

❖ Keep your outgoing message short – aim for no more than twenty seconds.

❖ Offer an explanation of why you are unavailable, or simply say, "We are unable to answer the phone right now."

❖ Never leave information on your voice mail that might cause security problems. It's not smart to brag, "We will be in the Bahamas until the end of the month."

❖ Encourage the caller to leave a message.

❖ If at all possible, provide an option for people to reach you personally if it is an emergency.

*Assure the Caller that you will return the call. Then keep your word.*

Finally, assure the caller that you will return the call. Then keep your word.

EXAMPLE: "Hello. This is the voice mail of Bill Davis. Please leave your message and I will return the call as soon as possible."

### *What is the correct way to leave a message on someone's voice mail.*

*RATHER THAN STATING, "CALL ME BACK," BE CLEAR ABOUT ANY SPECIFIC ACTION THE PERSON SHOULD TAKE BEFORE RETURNING THE CALL.*

This is not the time to record a long, detailed message. That's for when you are speaking personally.

- ❖ Begin your greeting with "Hello" or "Good afternoon."
- ❖ State your full name, phone number, and the purpose of your call.
- ❖ To avoid playing phone tag, let the person know when you can be reached (and always be available at that time).
- ❖ As with any answering system, keep your messages short and to the point.
- ❖ Rather than stating, "Call me back," be clear about any specific action the person should take before returning the call.
- ❖ Close with "Thank you," or "Good-bye" – never "Bye bye."

### *What is the most convenient manner of handling incoming voice mail messages?*

Follow the motto of the Boy Scouts: "Be Prepared." Always have a pen and note pad handy and take notes.

This is especially important regarding any follow-up action that may be necessary.

❖ Be sure to listen to the *entire* message. If you assume that you know what the person is about to say, you may be wrong. Far too often people think, "I know what he is going to say," and delete the message half way through.
❖ Check and clear your voice mail at least twice each day.
❖ Do not allow a message to remain on your voice mail for more than 24 hours.

Since leaving and retrieving electronic messages via voice mail and other devices will most likely be a part of your life forever, don't forget your manners in the digital world.

*CHECK AND CLEAR YOUR VOICE MAIL AT LEAST TWICE EACH DAY.*

# CALL WAITING

In our opinion, possibly no other electronic device has caused so much ill-mannered behavior as Call Waiting. It's the service you subscribe to that emits a beep when someone is attempting to phone you while you are on another call. What's the result? You interrupt your conversation to find out who is trying to reach you. And, by doing so, you are implying to the first caller, "This call is more important than you."

### *Should I ignore the Call Waiting signal?*

Only use this service when you are expecting an important call. The person you are speaking with is your priority, not another caller.

If you *do* use Call Waiting:

❖ At the start of the conversation, tell the caller, "I'm expecting a call from John Brown. If I have to leave the line for a moment, please excuse me."

❖ Always apologize to the original caller for an interruption.

❖ Make it a policy that you will rarely place your friends on hold.

❖ Never say, "I just received a very important call. I need to go now." That's impolite.

❖ If you are not expecting an important call, ignore the beep.

*NEVER SAY, "I JUST RECEIVED A VERY IMPORTANT CALL. I NEED TO GO NOW." THAT'S IMPOLITE.*

# CALLER ID

Millions of phones are equipped with Caller ID, a service that allows you to see the phone number (and in many areas, the *name*) of the person dialing. Most people use it to screen their calls.

Some are surprised when they call and the first words are,

"Hi, George!"

"How did you know it was me?" the caller responds.

"It says so right on my phone."

When using Caller ID, follow these rules:

- ❖ If you do not wish to speak to the person, let it go to your recorder or voice mail after three rings. However, always return a call when requested.
- ❖ Answer your phone with "Hello. This is (your full name)."
- ❖ Don't brag about your ID program to the caller.

Remember, some people have devices that automatically reject all calls from those who have blocked their caller ID. Know your phone's code for unblocking the system.

# TELEPHONE RULES TO REMEMBER

*A*fter discussing the contents of this chapter with members of your family, decide how your home phone will be used. The four most important concerns are:

*1. Set the hours and situations when you should and should not place or receive calls.*

*2. Determine the maximum length of time for calls.*

*3. Establish a specific style for receiving and placing calls.*

*ANSWER YOUR PHONE WITH "HELLO. THIS IS (YOUR FULL NAME)."*

*4. Have an official message-taking system.*

NOTE: Chapter Seven includes phone rules for children.

# RESPONDING TO TELEMARKETERS

### *Is there a polite way of dealing with unwanted phone solicitations?*

*M*ost telemarketers are sincere people who are trying to make a living. While you may not be interested in what they have to offer, treat them with kindness and avoid being rude. There is no reason to become angry or upset – it only results in interrupting your day.

Without being harsh or unkind, simply say, "Thanks for your call, but I'm not interested," then conclude the conversation.

Or, you may respond, "Would you please remove my name from your list? Thank you so much."

If the caller continues to talk, repeat the above response. Then politely conclude the call.

> *THERE IS NO REASON TO BECOME ANGRY OR UPSET – IT ONLY RESULTS IN INTERRUPTING YOUR DAY.*

# COMPUTER COURTESIES

*W*ith surprising speed, the computer has become an activity center in millions of homes. It is a source for news, business, entertainment, an educational treasure-trove, and the portal through which we view the world and keep in touch with our friends. However, like any valuable resource, sensible guidelines for its use need to be established.

### *What limits should be placed on the use of a home computer by family members?*

Computers can become addictive. Without realizing why, some individuals find themselves spending hundreds of hours every month glued to the monitor – chatting with friends, playing online games, or uncovering facts about their field of interest.

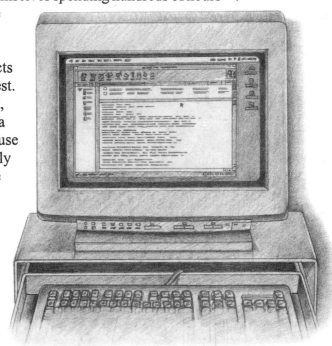

One father confessed, "We finally had to have a discussion and limit the use of the computer for family members. Otherwise, we would never have time for conversation."

Follow these guidelines:

❖ Like the phone, computer use (especially for chatting with

friends) should be limited to fifteen minutes.
- ❖ The computer should be a family resource, not dominated by one individual.
- ❖ Turn the monitor off during meals and other specified times.
- ❖ The audio volume should be kept low and not be allowed to interfere with others who may be nearby.

### Where should the home computer be located?

*T*he computer should be located in either the family room or the home office. Make sure the computer screen faces the center of the room. And, since parents should always monitor Internet use, do not place a computer in the bedroom of a child.

NOTE: Have a separate phone line for your Internet service, or purchase a piece of equipment that sends an incoming call to voice mail. It is frustrating to hear a busy signal for hours when someone ties up the phone line with a computer.

Later, in Chapter Seven, we will discuss how parents can help ensure their children have a positive computer experience.

*TO ERR IS HUMAN, BUT TO REALLY FOUL UP REQUIRES A COMPUTER.*

*– PAUL EHRLICH*

# TELEVISION ETIQUETTE

*A* study reported by the American Family Research Council found that parents spend less than 40 minutes each week in meaningful conversation with their children. Why such a small amount of time? The answer is found in one word: *television*.

The average child spends four hours every day watching television – and from birth to the age of 18 spends more time in front of a TV set than in the classroom.

Instead of allowing televison to dominate your home life, take a pro-active approach. For example, decide in advance what programs you will watch as a family each evening, and limit the number of hours the set is in use.

### Where should television sets be located in the home?

*I*deally, the television should be located in the family room. You may want additional sets in the kitchen and master bedroom.

We highly discourage placing a television in the bedroom of any child – even through the teen years. It not only isolates children from the family, but makes it almost impossible to monitor viewing habits. Plus, the television can interfere with both study time and sleep.

*INSTEAD OF ALLOWING TELEVISION TO DOMINATE YOUR LIFE, TAKE A PRO-ACTIVE APPROACH.*

*BY THE TIME CHILDREN COMPLETE ELEMENTARY SCHOOL, THE AVERAGE CHILD WILL WITNESS MORE THAN 100,000 ACTS OF VIOLENCE ON TV.*

*– CENTER FOR MEDIA EDUCATION*

For those occasions when your children are having a sleepover and want to watch a movie in their room, use a portable set equipped with a VCR or DVD.

### *How can television become a more positive influence on our family?*

Television is for either information or relaxation, and only you can decide how it should be used.

A family in South Carolina uses television news as a catalyst for family discussions. Said the mother, "At least one evening each week we watch a thirty-minute local newscast together. Then we turn off the set and spend another half hour discussing the day's local and national issues – even sports."

Many families decide in advance what programs they will watch. It's a wise move since the Center for Media Education states, "By the time children complete elementary school, the average child will witness more than 100,000 acts of violence on TV, including 8,000 murders."

To help make television watching a more positive experience, we recommend these rules:

❖ Don't turn on the television during meal times. It is an unnecessary distraction and takes away from family conversation.

❖ When watching, keep comments to a minimum so as not to disturb others. Wait until a commercial break to offer your opinions or questions.
❖ No member of the family should be allowed to "channel surf" when others are watching, unless, of course, if asked.
❖ Practice proper seating habits. For example, one person should not be allowed to "stretch out" on a sofa and deny seating to others.

Remember, television viewing is a family activity – and every member of your household is equally important.

### What television courtesies should be observed when guests are visiting our home?

f you invite friends to your home and are planning to watch a particular television program or movie, let them know in advance. They should accept or decline the invitation based on that information.

When guests enter the home, all family members should rise – even those who are watching a television program. It is also polite to turn off the set when friends arrive.

If you are a guest and wish to carry on a conversation with a particular family member, ask that person to leave the room. Don't disturb others.

*WHEN GUESTS ENTER THE HOME, ALL FAMILY MEMBERS SHOULD RISE – EVEN THOSE WHO ARE WATCHING A TELEVISION PROGRAM.*

### What etiquette issues involve electronic equipment?

*F*or reason of economics and safety, turn off the television set when not in use. If the monitor is in a cabinet, close the doors when not in use.

We recommend having a policy that you will not borrow or loan electronic equipment. Unforseen problems may arise that can cause ill will between friends. It's better to *give* a piece of used equipment than to loan it.

NOTE: When you check out media from a library or retail store, treat the videos and DVDs with respect. Always rewind videos, replace in the proper container and return before the due date.

## MUSIC MANNERS

*A* gentleman in Atlanta loved opera music so much that he piped it through a loud speaker system around the swimming pool in his backyard. There was only one problem. He turned up the volume so loud the neighbors two blocks away could hear it!

Soon there was a knock on the door from the local police. "What's wrong?" he wanted to know.

"Sir, if you don't turn down the volume, we will have to fine you for disturbing the peace."

*WE RECOMMEND HAVING A POLICY THAT YOU WILL NOT BORROW OR LOAN ELECTRONIC EQUIPMENT.*

## *What rules should be established for music at home?*

*J*ust because one member of your household enjoys a certain type of music – whether country, rock or classical – doesn't mean that others must be subjected to it day and night. That's why it is important to form a consensus regarding when, where, and how music is to be played in your home.

Here are guidelines worth adopting:

❖ The audio from Internet, radio, television or CDs should not be blasted throughout the home.
❖ The music volume should never interfere with normal conversation.
❖ Children and teens should not be allowed to wear stereo headsets at meal times or during other family activities.
❖ Specific time limits should be placed on music listening habits of children so that it will not interfere with homework or sleep.

Later in this book we will address the issue of music in public places and recommend specific guidelines for parents.

*THE MUSIC VOLUME SHOULD NEVER INTERFERE WITH NORMAL CONVERSATION.*

Chapter Three

# Today's Netiquette

The rules of common courtesy apply to every form of communication – whether it be in person, wired or wireless. Internet and e-mail users are certainly not immune. They've even coined a phrase for online etiquette – *netiquette.*

From e-mail to Instant Messaging, here are the principles and practices that will guide you to what is proper and acceptable when exchanging messages in cyberspace.

## E-Mail

Sending and receiving e-mail is no longer a novelty. It has become a primary means of communication for friends, families and businesses. In the workplace, it has virtually replaced the inter-office memo.

*We must learn to balance the material wonders of technology with the spiritual demands of our human nature.*

*– John Naisbitt*

Still, we need to ask: Is e-mail the most appropriate form for this message? Or should I send a fax or regular letter? For example, e-mail is *not* appropriate for:

❖ Sending or responding to formal invitations.
❖ A letter of condolence.
❖ A "thank you" letter for a gift or kindness.
❖ A formal contract, document or agreement.

A written response (whether typed or handwritten) conveys greater importance and is more highly valued than an e-mail.

### What are the basic rules for preparing an e-mail?

*T*he key to effective e-mail is to communicate simply and directly. People don't expect you to be an experienced writer, but they do want you to follow the rules.

Your letter should get to the point quickly and stick with the subject – don't wander. You should not have more than one or two topics in your e-mail.

Here are the basic guidelines to follow:

❖ If the message is informal, write casually. If it is serious, pay close attention to your word usage and grammar.
❖ Short paragraphs are better than long ones.

*THE KEY TO EFFECTIVE E-MAIL IS TO COMMUNI-CATE SIMPLY AND DIRECTLY.*

- ❖ An e-mail is not a telegram. Write in complete sentences.
- ❖ Do not write in all lowercase (or all uppercase) letters.
- ❖ Avoid the overuse of punctuation. Let your words provide the emphasis.
- ❖ If you are asking for a decision, include enough data for an appropriate response.
- ❖ Be careful about using satire or irony. The reader can't see your facial expressions, only your words.

*AVOID THE OVERUSE OF PUNCTUATION. LET YOUR WORDS PROVIDE THE EMPHASIS.*

Be specific about dates and times. Avoid saying "tomorrow" or "next Friday." You can't be certain when the e-mail will be read. Write Friday, June 28 at 3:00 p.m. Also, write the month as a word, not a number. In the U.S. 7/3/06 is July 3. In Europe the first two numbers are reversed so it would read March 7.

Your e-mail should convey the same courtesy used in everyday conversation. Remind yourself to say "thank you" and "please." Always use good taste and show respect for others.

### *What technical issues should I be concerned with?*

*S*tick to the basic ASCII (American Standard Code for Information Interchange) format used by nearly all e-mail programs. Other configurations may convert into gibberish. And limit the length of your lines to fewer than eighty characters. Otherwise, the recipient may see strange formatting and line breaks.

Remember these rules:

> ❖ Don't indent or use tabs since the receiver may not have the same format. Instead, add a line space and start the new paragraph flush left.
>
> ❖ Avoid using text art, color type or special backgrounds as part of your e-mail. The recipient's program may not be able to download them.
>
> ❖ Never type in all upper case letters. People will think you are shouting – plus, it is very difficult to read.
>
> ❖ Double check your grammar and spelling. If your e-mail program does not have a spell-checker, type the message in a word processor, check it, then copy to your e-mail program.
>
> ❖ Always read every word you type before you press the "send" key.

NOTE: Double check the name you are entering from your

*NEVER TYPE IN ALL UPPER CASE LETTERS. PEOPLE WILL THINK YOU ARE SHOUTING.*

address book. An e-mail sent to the person above or below the entry could be quite embarrassing.

### *What should be included in the subject line?*

Every e-mail should include a subject line. Never leave it blank. And make sure the subject accurately conveys the content of the message you are sending.

Avoid attention-getting symbols such as <<<<<<<<READ THIS NOW>>>>>>>>>> or "!!!!!!!!WOW!!!!!!!!!! Some people will think this is a commercial message, or consider you quite immature.

PROPER SUBJECT LINE: Requested Netiquette Guidelines.

### *What are the guidelines for sending to multiple recipients?*

Keep your target list rather short, and review your "CC" list regularly to add or delete names. Also, avoid sending e-mail to people who may not be interested.

NOTE: If you are sending messages to a large list of individuals who don't know each other, use BCC (Blind carbon copy). This will avoid your entire receiving list appearing on the message. When you use BCC, the recipient will see only his or her name and yours.

*EVERY E-MAIL SHOULD INCLUDE A SUBJECT LINE. NEVER LEAVE IT BLANK.*

### When is it appropriate to add a file attachment?

*A*void sending unsolicited attachments. Because of receiving a possible computer virus, some people never open them. Always send an e-mail in advance asking if the person would like to receive the attachment.

Only attach files if they are essential. They take time to download, use considerable memory on someone's computer, and often don't convert to the user's word processing program.

Also, when you *receive* an attachment, don't download it without running an anti-virus program. (Make sure a permanent anti-virus program is running on your computer at all times.)

### What is considered a proper "signature" for my e-mail?

*T*he information at the close of an e-mail – your signature – contains important data.

❖ Keep your signature short – three or four lines maximum.
❖ Include your full name, address, phone, fax, e-mail and any alternative means of reaching you.
❖ If you use a quote or humorous phrase as part of

---

*KEEP YOUR SIGNATURE SHORT – THREE OR FOUR LINES MAXIMUM.*

your signature, keep the item short – and be sure no one may be offended by it.
❖ Change clever sayings often. After several e-mails they are no longer amusing.

IMPROPER SIGNATURE: National League of Cotillions. "Always treat others with honor, dignity and respect."
PROPER SIGNATURE:
National League of Cotillions.
Mail: P.O. Box 204384, Charlotte, NC 28224.
Phone: 1-800-633-7947.
Fax: 1-704-864-3232. E-mail: cotillions@nljc.com.
Internet: www.nljc.com.

Also, try to avoid signatures that build a picture out of keyboard characters. They usually become mangled on someone else's system.

### *What guidelines should be observed when replying to an e-mail message?*

*M*ake it a personal rule that you will not reply to an original message more than once. When you keep adding comments to the "threads," the message can become confusing.

*Make it a personal rule that you will not reply to an original message more than once.*

-69-

*NEVER RESPOND QUICKLY TO AN E-MAIL THAT UPSETS YOU. IF YOU FEEL ANNOYED OR ANGRY, WAIT AT LEAST ONE DAY TO REPLY.*

Some e-mails also have files attached which can take up precious memory space. It is better to send a new e-mail than to resend extremely long or multiple messages.

Here are additional rules for replying:

❖ Respond as soon as possible to the e-mail messages you receive.

❖ Change the subject line to match your reply.

❖ Some people send so many e-mails, they may not remember the content of what they sent. Always refer to the most important issue of the original message as a reminder to the sender in your reply.

❖ If the person has spent considerable time sending you a message, it is discourteous to give a curt reply such as "Ditto," or "I agree." Write at least one or two full paragraphs.

❖ Never respond quickly to an e-mail that upsets you. If you feel annoyed or angry, wait at least one day to reply.

❖ Place the symbol > before quoted text.

Also, do not reply to an entire list unless your answer is of interest (and applies) to all. And don't edit a quoted message. The meaning could be changed and the original writer offended.

NOTE: When you receive an important e-mail, give a quick

response that it has been received – and let the person know approximately when you will be replying. If your computer crashes, don't use this as an excuse for not communicating. Reply instead by phone, fax, or overnight letter.

### What are the rules regarding the forwarding of e-mail?

ou should not forward an e-mail without permission of the original sender. And if you only forward a portion of an e-mail, add a note to explain what you have done.

For privacy reasons, always delete the distribution list before forwarding.

Here's a word of caution: *Never be tempted to forward a get-rich-quick scheme, a conspiracy theory, or a chain letter.*

### Should I be concerned with e-mail privacy?

*A*ssume the e-mail administrators of your web server have the ability to read your messages – because they do! And be aware that many companies monitor the e-mail messages of their employees, Assume they may read yours.

Also, remember that it is possible for "hackers" to read your e-mail. Some people do it for fun.

Finally, never use your personal or business credit card number with an e-mail message.

*You should not forward an e-mail without permission of the original sender.*

### What is meant by an e-mail "flame"?

*I*n the invisible electronic world, some people become upset when your etiquette does not meet their standards. They may even respond by sending a rather hot message – called a "flame."

Who can expect a negative response?
- ❖ The person who writes in ALL CAPS. You'll be accused of "shouting."
- ❖ The sender of an unsolicited mass mailing.
- ❖ The person who makes a comment about someone's grammar, spelling or punctuation.

What should you do if you receive such a reply? If it is from someone you don't know, ignore it. You don't want to get into a "flame war." If it comes from a friend, reply and apologize if necessary.

*IF YOU RECEIVE A "FLAME" FROM SOMEONE YOU DON'T KNOW, IGNORE IT.*

### How should I handle unsolicited "Spam" e-mail?

*I*t is futile to become upset and attempt to contact the sender. Instead, discuss the matter with your Internet service provider. They will help you install an anti-spam filter. The same issue regards "pop-up" advertising that is an invasion of your privacy. Free programs such as *POP-UP STOPPER* (www.panicware.com) are excellent for reducing the problem.

# INSTANT MESSAGING

*W*ithout question, the preferred choice of distance communication among teens is Instant Messaging (IM). And it has spread to millions of other age users worldwide.

People like it because it's lightning-quick. The questions and answers are exchanged in "real time" and you are actually in a real conversation.

While e-mail is great for sending memos and files, IM is best for short messages and fast responses.

There are many benefits:

❖ You are in control of who you converse with.
❖ You can set your online schedule.
❖ It's possible to take a break. You can't do that during a phone call.
❖ It allows you to keep in touch with your friends and relatives.
❖ You can talk and do several other computer-related tasks at once.
❖ You can engage in multiple conversations at the same time.
❖ It decreases phone bills for those who communicate at a distance.

*WHILE E-MAIL IS GREAT FOR SENDING MEMOS AND FILES, INSTANT MESSAGING IS BEST FOR SHORT MESSAGES AND FAST RESPONSES.*

### *What courtesies should I observe when working with my "buddy list"?*

*W*ith AOL's Instant Messenger software, Yahoo!, Microsoft's MSN Messenger and other programs, you set up a contact list or "buddy list" of those with whom you frequently communicate. From the names, you can instantly see who is online. It also helps create an environment that is safe.

Some individuals have more than one hundred people entered on their list. Your "buddy" directory should not be used to make new friends, but to keep in contact with those you have.

> *BE TRUTHFUL. IF YOU CLICK THE ICONS "AVAILABLE" OR "ONLINE," MAKE CERTAIN YOU REALLY ARE.*

- ❖ Be truthful. If you click the icons "Available" or "Online," make certain you really are. Also, if you click "Busy" or "Do not disturb," that should also be the fact.
- ❖ If someone is marked "Away," don't pester him or her.
- ❖ Allow a person off-line time to respond. He or she may want to talk later.
- ❖ If you are sending messages across the country, know the time zones. Don't be online when a person is sleeping or having meals.

### What's the best way to start and end messages?

$\mathcal{B}$egin by requesting the person's time. "Do you have a minute?" "Can we chat?" Or, "Are you busy?"

End with, "I need to sign off." Or, "That's it for now."

### What are the benefits of Instant Messaging in the business environment?

$\mathcal{T}$he number of corporations and small businesses using this form of communication continues to grow. Why?

- ❖ It is ideal for a group of people in different locations who are working on the same task.
- ❖ Organizations find it an inexpensive way to stay in touch with staff who are on the road.
- ❖ It's great for informal communications. (Avoid using for formal requests, since it doesn't have an aura of significance.)

*INSTANT MESSAGING IS AN INEXPENSIVE WAY TO STAY IN TOUCH WITH STAFF WHO ARE ON THE ROAD.*

# ABBREVIATIONS AND SYMBOLS

$\mathcal{N}$etiquette has developed its own unique codes of communication. The abbreviations and symbols below are sometimes used in informal e-mail between friends and family.

We present this list to help you understand some of the messages you may receive, not as a recommendation for your writing style.

*USE SYMBOLS AND ABBREV- IATIONS SPARINGLY.*

| | | | |
|---|---|---|---|
| AFAIK | – As far as I know. | NM | – Never mind, or no matter. |
| BBL | – Be back later. | | |
| BBS | – Be back soon. | NP | – No problem. |
| BRB | – Be right back. | OBO | – Or best offer. |
| BTW | – By the way. | OIC | – Oh, I see. |
| BF | – Boy friend. | OMG | – Oh my gosh! |
| GF | – Girl friend. | PM | – Private message. |
| GFN | – Gone for now. | PMFJI | – Pardon me for jumping in. |
| GTG | – Got to go. | | |
| H&K | – Hug and kiss. | SYS | – See you soon. |
| HAGN | – Have a good night. | TA | – Thanks again. |
| IMHO | – In my humble opinion. | TTFN | – Ta ta for now. |
| | | TTYL | – Talk to you later. |
| JK | – Just kidding. | TY | – Thank you. |
| LOL | – Laughing out loud. | WB | – Welcome back. |
| LY | – Love ya! | YW | – You're welcome. |

## I've seen a few typographical symbols on my e-mails. What do they mean?

*S*ome writers use a few keystrokes to create "smileys."

Since they express human emotion, others call them "emoticons." If you turn your head to the left you will see the face of the smiley. These symbols are usually placed at the end of a sentence and refer to what's been said. Here are a few examples:

| | |
|---|---|
| :-) | Happy face. |
| ;-) | Wink. |
| :-I | Indifference. |
| :-> | Devilish grin. |
| 8-) | Eyeglasses. |
| :-D | Shock or surprise. |
| :-p | Sticking out your tongue (only to close friends). |
| :-/ | Perplexed. |
| :-( | Frown or displeasure. |
| :-@ | Scream. |
| :-O | Yell. |

Also, placing the "greater-smaller" keystrokes around a word can indicate emotion: <sigh> <grin>.

We recommend you use these symbols sparingly – or not at all. To most people, they are signs of a new e-mail writer, or someone trying to be humorous. Whenever possible, convey your thoughts with words, not symbols.

*WHENEVER POSSIBLE, CONVEY YOUR THOUGHTS WITH WORDS, NOT SYMBOLS.*

*THE STYLE IN WHICH YOU COMMUNI-CATE WITH E-MAIL AND INSTANT MESSAGING IS A REFLECTION OF YOUR CHARACTER AND PERSONALITY.*

### How can I emphasize words when there is no underline keystroke available?

*H*ere's how many e-mail users solve the problem. To emphasize a word or a phrase, surround it with "stars." Example: "I *warned* you not to tell her!"

Also, since e-mail does not have an underlining feature, you can surround your type with the underscore symbol to indicate it: Example: _ Gone _With _ the _ Wind _. Some writers use hyphens: Gone-With-the-Wind.

~

*T*he style in which you communicate with e-mail and Instant Messaging is a reflection of your character and personality. Make certain you treat your unseen friends with admiration and respect.

# CHAPTER FOUR

# ELECTRONIC ETIQUETTE AT THE OFFICE

*H*ow times have changed! In the early 1900s there were only two or three telephones for every one hundred people – and that included businesses.

It didn't make any difference whether you managed the local bank, ran the hardware store or lived on a farm: The only way to make a call was to walk up to a wall-mounted wooden box, lift the receiver and hope no one else was talking. If all was clear, you would wind the crank to get the attention of the operator at the central phone office.

There was absolutely no privacy. Every line was shared with at least eight parties, and you could listen in on conversations anytime you wanted.

Yet, even then phone etiquette was important. In 1914, the telephone company in Elkhorn, Wisconsin, published these

*IN THE EARLY 1900S...YOU COULD LISTEN IN ON CONVER- SATIONS ANYTIME YOU WANTED.*

guidelines for its 600 subscribers:

1. *Calls are limited to three minutes.*
2. *No party should hold the line for longer than five minutes.*
3. *Do not take down receiver when others are using the line.*
4. *Don't waste the operator's time in useless talk.*
5. *If you will "ring off," the operator will not have to listen to know when you are through.*

Just imagine conducting business on the phone under those circumstances!

Today, the number of telephones is in the *billions*. And without the ability of instant communication, world business would come to a grinding halt.

Here's a guide to telephone etiquette and manners in today's workplace.

*WITHOUT THE ABILITY OF INSTANT COMMUNICATION, WORLD BUSINESS WOULD COME TO A GRINDING HALT.*

# ANSWERING THE BUSINESS PHONE

The manager of a computer warehouse called his office when he was out of the city and was shocked when the receptionist answered abruptly, "Hang on! I'm placing you on hold!"

There was no, "Good afternoon. Global Computers, this is Mary. How can I help you?"

The manager was tempted to give the employee an instant lecture, but instead he called a staff meeting the next day and set the rules for how company phones were to be answered.

The first voice heard by a caller becomes the image of the organization. Since first impressions are lasting, it is extremely important that the person chosen to answer the phone is personable, well-trained and professional.

Regardless of the size of your organization and the complexity of the communication system, there are three basics we should never forget:

1. Every caller should be treated with sincere courtesy and respect.
2. Callers should be connected to real people as quickly as possible, not a maze of voice message choices.
3. The requests of every caller should be met.

Now let's look at the ways these objectives are accomplished.

### How should a receptionist or secretary properly answer the office phone?

Immediately, in a positive, professional tone, say "Good morning, National League of Cotillions, Suzanne speaking. How may I help you?"

Be as polite and helpful as possible. If the caller asks, "I'd

*How well we communicate is determined not by how well we say things, but by how well we are understood.*

*– Andy S. Grove*

like to speak with Mr. Winters," respond with, "May I tell him who is calling please?"

If you do not recognize the caller, inquire: "May I ask what this pertains to?"

Never tell the caller, "He's out for coffee," or "He's at the doctor's office." That is personal information people do not need to know. If the person is out of the office, say so before asking who is calling. Don't give the impression you are screening calls.

Should the person being called not be available, say, "Would you like for me to transfer you to his (or her) voice mail, or would you like for me to take a message?" Often, the caller will prefer that you create a handwritten message (See "Taking and Leaving Messages" in Chapter Two).

*If You Do Not Recognize the Caller, Inquire, "May I ask What This Pertains To?"*

### How should employees in various departments receive a call?

It is best to answer by giving your full name – and even your department. "Hello, this is Customer Relations, John Morgan speaking." Use your name, but not your title.

If your message is on voice mail, say: "You've reached the voice mail of John Morgan in Customer Relations. Please leave your message and phone number. I will return your call as soon as possible. Thank you." Make sure your tone is warm and friendly.

### *How should I respond if an important call arrives while I have a visitor in my office?*

*Y*our guest should always take priority. If the call is of an emergency nature, ask the guest to remain in your office while you go to another location. Keep the phone conversation short and return as quickly as possible.

If you are the guest when such a call comes in, offer to exit the room so the person can have privacy. Should you be asked to remain, direct your attention to something else while the person completes the call.

### *What are the guidelines for answering someone's office phone?*

*T*here may be times you are requested to take calls for someone else. When that happens:

❖ Answer by saying, "Bob Smith's line, John Brown speaking."
❖ Explain the reason you are answering the phone.
❖ Don't make a promise that the person will call

*WHETHER ON THE PHONE OR IN PERSON, PEOPLE SHOULD BE TREATED WITH ESTEEM AND RESPECT.*

*– SARA SEIBERLING, COTILLION DIRECTOR, NASHVILLE, TN*

back. You can only say, "Thank you. I will give him the message."

❖ Be careful when speaking about a colleague. Avoid saying, "He's in the restroom," or "She's still having lunch."

*DON'T FEEL YOU MUST SPEAK IMMEDIATELY TO EVERY PERSON TRYING TO REACH YOU.*

### How can I avoid spending too much time receiving calls?

If you're not careful, the telephone can dominate your schedule. Here are ways to avoid that trap:

❖ Have frequent discussions with your receptionist or secretary regarding how you want your calls screened.

❖ Don't feel you must speak immediately to every person trying to reach you.

❖ Never hesitate to tell a caller, up front, that you only have five minutes.

❖ Avoid becoming too personal or familiar with first time callers.

❖ Organize your time by having specific hours to take and return phone calls.

# Transferring Calls

*S*ome calls are best handled by another person and the caller needs to be transferred. You can smooth the process by following these rules:

- ❖ Begin by offering your assistance.
- ❖ Give the reason you cannot answer the question. Ask permission to transfer the caller to someone who can help.
- ❖ Only transfer the call if you feel certain the particular person will be of assistance.
- ❖ Reassure the individual: "I believe Mrs. Grant will be able to assist you."
- ❖ Give the caller both the name and number of the person you are transferring them to.
- ❖ Stay on the line until the new party answers – or until you know the call has been switched to voice mail. Then quietly place the receiver down.

Also, never forward an office call to someone's residence without first notifying that person. Without such permission, you are invading his or her privacy.

*Only transfer the call if you feel the particular person will be of assistance.*

# PLACING CALLERS ON HOLD

*I*n a busy office, placing someone on hold is often un-avoidable. In such situations:

> ❖ When possible, ask for permission to place the person on hold. If the caller is not pleased, or it is going to be more than five minutes, request a number where you can return the call.
>
> ❖ Let the caller know why he or she is being placed on hold.
>
> ❖ Don't be brusque and say, "Hold on!"
>
> ❖ If you place someone on hold, come back to him or her with a progress report at least every 30 seconds.
>
> ❖ The first caller should be given priority.

EXAMPLE: If you are on the phone, have your secretary say, "Mr. Black is on another call at the moment. May I ask him to call you back or would you like to be placed on hold?"

Remember to say "Thanks for waiting" when you return to the line with the information requested by the caller.

NOTE: If a senior executive is calling, always have a signal system in place to let your boss know.

Also, If music is used on the line, be certain it reflects your company's image. Soft instrumental music is usually best. (Always avoid music with lyrics.)

*LET THE CALLER KNOW WHY HE OR SHE IS BEING PLACED ON HOLD.*

# OFFICE ANSWERING MACHINES

*W*hen it is impossible to personally answer your office phone, leave a recorded message. For an effective greeting:

❖ Let the caller know your first and last name and the office they have reached.
❖ Make sure your voice is warm, positive and enthusiastic.
❖ Invite the caller to leave his or her phone number and promise to call back.
❖ State the hours your office is open (or when someone will be answering in person).

Remember, how you answer the phone on your machine is just as important as how you would answer in person. You are making a lasting impression.

Check your messages several times each day – even if that means access from a remote location. Keep a pad and paper handy to note phone numbers and any action you must take. Make it a habit to delete answering machine messages immediately. Only save a message that contains details someone else needs to hear.

*How you answer the phone on your machine is just as important as how you would answer in person.*

### *What rules should I follow when leaving a message?*

*L*et the person know who is calling and what organization you represent. Keep your message short. Speak clearly and slowly. Let people know the best time to call you back. Always repeat your name and number twice and conclude with a courtesy – "Thanks" or "Thank you."

# HANDLING RUDE OR ANGRY CALLERS

*STAY CALM AND POLITE, REGARDLESS OF HOW UPSET THE CALLER IS.*

### *What should be my response to someone who is extremely upset?*

*I*f you work in an organization long enough you will probably receive a call from an individual who is agitated and irate. When that happens:

- ❖ Stay calm and polite, regardless of how upset the caller is.
- ❖ Ask, "Would you repeat that slowly so I can write it down?"
- ❖ Listen carefully and express, "I understand what you are saying."
- ❖ Convey your heartfelt desire to resolve the issue.

❖ If you feel the matter is important, arrange to have a company executive call back shortly. Then follow through to make sure that happens.

❖ Never argue.

❖ If you or your organization is at fault, don't hesitate to admit it.

❖ If necessary, apologize and quickly correct the problem.

❖ Thank the caller for bringing the matter to your attention.

❖ Conclude on a positive note.

Remember, solving the callers's problem or answering his or her request is the key to effective customer relations in your organization.

*YOU RESPECT AN EXECUTIVE'S SCHEDULE BY KEEPING YOUR CALLS BRIEF.*

# PLACING BUSINESS CALLS

*T*he key to placing successful calls to any organization is the word *respect*.

❖ You *respect* an executive's schedule by keeping your calls brief.

❖ You *respect* a person's office or position by making the individual feel valued and admired.

❖ You *respect* a person's dignity by not engaging in gossip or using offensive language.

### *What are the rules to follow when calling a business executive?*

*W*atch the clock and observe time zones. Calls to offices should be made between 9:00 A.M. and noon, and from 2:00 P.M. to 4:00 P.M. The exception to the 9:00 A.M. time is Monday morning – that's when many companies have staff meetings. On that day, call after 10:00 A.M.

Also, avoid calling near closing time. At the end of the day employees are often tired, busy organizing their paperwork and not mentally ready for your intrusion.

Here are additional guidelines:

❖ When calling an organization, immediately identify yourself and the company you are representing. For example, "This is Bob King with IBM. May I speak with Mr. Walters?" This helps the secretary know who is calling.

❖ Make friends with the secretary. Learn her name and, if possible, compliment her since she can be of great help. Be sincere in your comments.

❖ If it is impossible to speak with the person immediately, share the nature of your request with the secretary. Ask her to schedule a convenient time to speak with the executive.

*WHEN CALLING AN ORGANIZATION, IMMEDIATELY IDENTIFY YOURSELF AND THE COMPANY YOU REPRESENT.*

❖ Unless it is an emergency, do not call the executive at home.

NOTE: If someone (such as an assistant) places a call on your behalf, be available to speak immediately. Never keep the recipient waiting.

### *How can I add personality to my business calls?*

*A* woman who runs a day care center in Dallas keeps her Rolodex next to her phone. If a customer says, "We're taking a vacation to Arizona next month," she jots a note on the card. You can rest assured that the next time she calls that individual she will ask, "By the way, how was your trip to Arizona? Did you get to the Grand Canyon?"

People love it when you remember the details of their lives. Don't trust your memory – write it down! Let your next conversation reflect on the past, then move forward.

Your phone calls should include more than data and facts. To add warmth:

❖ Frequently use the name of the person. "Mary, that's an excellent idea!"

❖ Ask questions that touch on family, sports or community happenings. "Is Johnny still collecting baseball cards?" "How is Tiffany coming along with her gymnastics?"

*PEOPLE LOVE IT WHEN YOU REMEMBER THE DETAILS OF THEIR LIVES.*

❖ Use polite expressions. "Please" and "Thank you" are still in style.
❖ Look for opportunities to pay compliments.
❖ Smile as you speak.
❖ Use vocal variety – avoid a monotone voice.

Avoid topics of politics, religion or finances unless that is the intended purpose of the call.

### What privacy issues should concern me?

*N*ever pick up an extension phone and listen in on a conversation. And do not discuss confidential matters in an area where you can be overheard. Instead, move to a conference room.

# BUSINESS VOICE MAIL

*I*n the previous chapter we discussed voice mail at home. Many of those same rules apply at the office – plus more.

Make it your objective to become a master of your company's voice mail system. You'll be surprised at what you can accomplish – such as transferring a message into the voice mail of a fellow employee.

*Y*OUR WORDS HAVE SPECIAL MEANING WHEN SPOKEN WITH A SMILE.

– CINDY OATES, COTILLION DIRECTOR, WILMINGTON, NC

## *How can I make the most effective use of my voice mail?*

*U*pdate the message on your system daily, and sometimes even more often. Don't hesitate to give details of when you will return. For example, "This is Martha. I'll be at a conference until three o'clock this afternoon and will return your call before I leave the office."

Here are more rules to follow:

❖ Arrange to have a "live person" as an option. Say, "If you need help immediately, please call Howard Jones at extension 578."

❖ If you are away from your desk, program your calls to transfer to your voice mail quickly. Otherwise, a fellow employee may think it is necessary to pick up your phone.

❖ Never allow your voice mailbox to overflow. It doesn't make you look busy, just unorganized.

❖ Become known as a person who returns calls promptly.

Make it a habit to check your outgoing message frequently. You're not making a good impression if your message says, "I'll be back at 2:30 on Monday the 10th," and it is already Wednesday the 12th.

*BECOME KNOWN AS A PERSON WHO RETURNS CALLS PROMPTLY.*

### What's considered good etiquette for leaving messages on someone's business voice mail?

First, don't sound exasperated or upset because you could not reach the person. There's usually a good reason he or she is away from the phone.

Next, never leave more than three messages to the same individual. After that, you become a nuisance.

Finally, let your personality come through the phone. When you smile, it can be heard in your voice.

## CONFERENCE CALLS

Speakerphones have dramatically increased the scheduling of calls with multiple participants. With good equipment, excellent preparation and an awareness of conference call etiquette, the session will be productive.

### What is the protocol for phone conversations when several people are participating?

Successful conference calls require planning. Ask the participants to arrive a few minutes early so that you can talk

*NEVER LEAVE MORE THAN THREE MESSAGES TO THE SAME INDIVIDUAL. AFTER THAT, YOU BECOME A NUISANCE.*

about the call before it begins. Make sure every participant has a chair and a notepad, and that all needed documents and materials are in place. Then start the call two or three minutes ahead of schedule to ensure the connection is working and to get "small talk" out of the way.

Here are additional suggestions to make the sessions more effective:

❖ Be sure to identify every person who is in the room.
❖ Each time you speak, identify yourself.
❖ Have a schedule and stick to it.
❖ A phone with a headset may be helpful for the moderator.
❖ Keep paper shuffling to a minimum.
❖ Should only one person need to speak, pressing the *mute* button will help cancel background noise.
❖ During the call, always turn off the Call Waiting option on your phone.

Remember to avoid putting your phone on hold during the call. It can cause technical problems. Also, try not to use wireless or cordless phones since they often produce distracting noises.

*START THE CALL TWO OR THREE MINUTES AHEAD OF SCHEDULE TO MAKE SURE THE CONNECTION IS WORKING AND TO GET "SMALL TALK" OUT OF THE WAY.*

### Should speakerphones be used for one-on-one calls?

*D*o your best to avoid using the speakerphone for personal calls. They pick up background noise and you sound as if you are in an echo chamber. However, there may be occasions when a speakerphone is helpful – for example, when you need to leave your desk to retrieve some documents.

*Do Your Best to Avoid Using the Speaker- phone for Personal Calls.*

## VIDEO CONFERENCES

*T*he president of a college in Pennsylvania with a branch campus in Atlanta said, "We were spending thousands of dollars for plane tickets and hotel rooms flying executives back and forth for planning sessions before switching to video conferences." He added, "The meetings via television are extremely productive and the man-hours saved has been enormous."

### What preparations are needed to make the video conference more effective?

*B*efore the conference practice with the system and test your visuals. Prepare your graphics with large type since television monitors may be small.

Prior to the video event, follow these guidelines:

❖ Send presentation materials to participants as handouts.

❖ Create a checklist, an agenda and time schedule.

❖ Rehearse basic camera shots.

❖ Establish your backup should the system fail.

❖ Prepare name cards (with bold letters) for each participant.

Also, pay attention to what you wear. Choose solid color clothing – no patterns or stripes. Avoid blacks and dark reds. Pastel shirts and blouses are better than white. Women should not use very red lipstick or heavy eye makeup.

*CREATE A CHECKLIST, AN AGENDA AND TIME SCHEDULE.*

### What protocol should I follow during the video conference?

*If* you are the leader, make certain you start on time and

introduce all participants at each site. Don't worry about the delay in transmission (usually only one second).

Follow these rules:

- ❖ Start on time and introduce all participants.
- ❖ Always speak in the direction of a microphone.
- ❖ Look directly into the camera for eye contact.
- ❖ Ask plenty of questions and show personal interest in every participant.
- ❖ Move slowly so that the camera does not lose you.
- ❖ There should be only one speaker at a time.
- ❖ Allow time for a wrap-up.

A FINAL WORD: Since you never know when you're on camera, avoid nervous habits such as scratching your head or tapping your fingers. And throw out the gum!

## OFFICE COMPUTER ETIQUETTE

*H*enry hadn't been at his desk for two minutes when a colleague asked, "How was the party last night?"

"What party?" Henry answered, rather surprised. "How did you know about that?"

"Well, that was the message you left on your computer before you left yesterday," replied the associate.

What was Henry's mistake? He was working in an environment where more than one employee shared the same

*A*SK
PLENTY OF
QUESTIONS
AND SHOW
PERSONAL
INTEREST IN
EVERY
PARTICIPANT.

computer and he failed to log off properly.

Here are rules to follow at the office:

❖ Guard your privacy. Assume that all of your messages may be read by associates.

❖ Respect confidentiality. Should you accidentally see a file that is personal, avoid reading the contents and notify the person that the record exists.

❖ Practice a "strictly business" policy. Make a personal commitment that the office computer will be used for company use only.

# LAPTOP MANNERS

Company executive meetings have changed. Instead of a group of managers seated at a table with notepads, now there are laptops.

When using a portable computer in the presence of others:

❖ Turn the volume control to "mute."

❖ *Never* check your e-mail, pull up an Internet site, play an electronic game or work on a file unrelated to the purpose of the meeting.

❖ Assume those next to you can read your laptop screen.

For security reasons, don't leave your portable computer unsecured. If the room is not locked during a lunch break, take

*Make a Personal Commitment that the Office Computer will be used for Company Use Only.*

the laptop with you.

# HAND-HELD DEVICES

*P*ersonal electronic organizers such as the Palm Pilot are used by millions. They help keep our schedule on track and connect us with the world. At the office, however, we need to make certain their use is appropriate. For example, if you are the only person in a business meeting with a hand-held organizer, refrain from its use. It can become a distraction or, worse, you may be seen as a show-off.

Regardless of how dull the meeting may be, don't use your personal organizer to check messages or write notes about other issues. Also, avoid "playing" with your organizer or checking out its features.

If you need to exchange data with an associate using your hand-held device, wait until the meeting concludes. You show your respect to others by giving your full attention to the topic at hand.

In Chapter Five we will discuss proper manners for using copy machines and office printers.

*YOU SHOW YOUR RESPECT TO OTHERS BY GIVING YOUR FULL ATTENTION TO THE TOPIC AT HAND.*

# FAX, COPIER AND PRINTER PROTOCOL

At the start of the electronic age, headlines read, "Paperless Society in Our Future." Well, it did not happen.

In many respects, the *opposite* has taken place. Fax machines download millions of documents every day and the proliferation of copiers and printers is unprecedented.

This chapter is a guide to manners when using this special equipment.

## FAX ETIQUETTE

The advent of the fax machine had a dramatic effect on the transfer of documents. Suddenly huge numbers of abstracts, records and reports were being instantly transferred between offices and homes around the world. Many people thought the

*ONE OF THE GREATEST VICTORIES YOU CAN GAIN OVER A MAN IS TO BEAT HIM AT POLITENESS.*

*– JOSH BILLINGS*

~

arrival of e-mail would replace this technology; however, there are situations when sending a fax is the best choice.

Here is how you can make the most of your fax correspondence.

### *What are the basic rules to follow when faxing?*

*I*f you send faxes frequently, you'll first need to get organized. Set up an area near your fax machine with cover sheets, pens, paper, etc. Follow these rules:

- ❖ Don't assume everyone has a fax machine. Inquire politely if you need to send a fax.
- ❖ If the document is of special importance, make a quick phone call to confirm its receipt.
- ❖ It is always courteous to call before sending a long document. Avoid sending a lengthy fax during peak hours.
- ❖ Be aware that sending a long fax will tie up someone's machine. Consider sending those via e-mail or regular mail.
- ❖ Double check your dialing digits before sending. One number difference could send your fax to Nairobi instead of New Orleans.
- ❖ Avoid sending a fax in the middle of the night to someone's home. The noise can be disturbing.

*DON'T ALLOW A WIRELESS WORLD TO SUBSTITUTE FOR PERSONAL RELATION-SHIPS.*

*– JOAN SNODGRASS, COTILLION DIRECTOR, AUSTIN, TX*

Wait until daytime.

❖ Disable your "call waiting" if it is tied to the same phone that uses the fax machine. Otherwise there may be a disruption.

❖ Limit the size of a fax to a standard 8 ½" x 11" page. Try to avoid sending legal-size sheets or they may not be received properly.

Finally, never send unsolicited faxes. You are imposing an expense on the recipients by wasting their paper and toner.

*Follow this Fax rule: Read twice and send once.*

### *What concerns should I have regarding the content of a fax?*

The manager of an employment agency gave this advice: "A carpenter always measures twice and cuts once. The same rule should apply to faxes: read twice and send once." It's important to check punctuation, grammar and spelling before you send a document.

Some other guidelines:

❖ Never read faxes meant for other people. It is an invasion of privacy –

> *THE REAL DANGER IS NOT THAT MACHINES WILL BEGIN TO THINK LIKE MEN, BUT THAT MEN WILL BEGIN TO THINK LIKE MACHINES.*
>
> *– SYDNEY J. HARRIS*

like opening mail or listening to a phone call.

❖ Avoid sending jokes to a public fax machine. Someone is sure to be offended.

❖ Do not send business correspondence from your home. If you do, use a personal cover sheet.

❖ Never send a private message to or from a public office via fax. Assume everyone will read it.

### What details should a fax cover sheet include?

Never send a fax without a cover sheet. It should be simple, easy-to-read, with very few graphics. Be sure it includes:

❖ The date the fax is being sent.

❖ The name (and organization) of the person sending.

❖ The name of the recipient.

❖ The fax and phone numbers of both parties (should you need to confirm that the fax has been received).

❖ Brief description of what the fax contains.

❖ The number of pages being sent.

❖ Your letterhead should include additional contact information.

Here's a sample:

> *Avoid Fancy Borders and Intricate Logos. Keep the Graphics Simple.*

### How can I improve the graphics in a fax transmission?

*I*'m sure you have received faxes with photos that look like the inside of a train tunnel – almost solid black. Keep the graphics simple. Intricate logos and fancy borders slow transmission, increase your phone bills, and look unsightly to the recipient.

Here's how to help remedy graphics problems:

- ❖ If your fax contains photos, test it on "copy" to see what it will look like when transmitted.
- ❖ Either eliminate the photos or make copies with a "light" setting until the photos duplicate clearly.
- ❖ Line drawings transmit much better than photos.
- ❖ Heavy dark areas take far too much time to send – and waste toner.
- ❖ Understand that "whiteout" touch up can look like a blotch to the recipient.
- ❖ Avoid using colored paper. (If the original is on colored paper, photocopy it first in black and white.)
- ❖ Use readable type – perhaps enlarging before transmission.

With planning and practice, your faxes will both communicate your message and enhance your image.

*WITH PLANNING AND PRACTICE, YOUR FAXES WILL BOTH COMMUNICATE YOUR MESSAGE AND ENHANCE YOUR IMAGE.*

## COPY MACHINE MANNERS

*Y*ou're in a hurry! In a few minutes you have an important meeting and need to make just one duplicate of a needed document. However, when you reach the copy machine, someone with a stack of books two feet high is using the copier – and is treating it as exclusive territory.

When that happens, don't hesitate to ask, "Do you know how long you'll be using the machine? I just need to make one copy!"

Whether using a copier at a library, office supply store or at your place of employment, always treat others as you would like to be treated.

### *What etiquette issues should I be aware of when using the copier?*

It's important to always stay near the machine while making copies. You never know when an emergency will arise. If the copier has a paper jam, don't simply walk away and expect the next user to solve the problem. Notify a supervisor immediately.

Here are other rules to follow:

❖ Be considerate of others. Never make more than 25 or 30 copies when someone is standing in line behind you.
❖ Never leave the machine empty. Learn how to refill the paper tray.
❖ After making your last copy, clear the machine of

*THE COPY MACHINE GOLDEN RULE: ALWAYS TREAT OTHERS AS YOU WOULD LIKE TO BE TREATED.*

*THE COPY
MACHINE
AREA AT YOUR
WORKPLACE
IS NOT A
CONVER-
SATION
PLACE.
SAVE THE
SOCIALIZING
FOR
LUNCHTIME
OR FOR
AFTER-
HOURS.*

all special instructions (paper size, zoom, number of copies, etc.). The next user should have a  machine set at standard settings.
❖ Always remember to remove your original copy.

A final word. The copy machine area at your workplace is not a conversation place. Save the socializing for lunchtime or for after-hours.

# PRINTER PROTOCOL

In most offices, printers are a shared resource, usually connected to many computer users. For that reason, we need to be sensitive to the needs of others.

Don't feel you need to print out every page of a computer file. Take the time to view every document online and print only the material necessary. And since printers usually wear out faster than copy machines, avoid using the printer for making multiple copies.

### *What printer-related issues should I be concerned with?*

Your objective should be to see that the work flows smoothly and that you do not monopolize use of the printer.

❖ Don't tie up the printer for hours. Print just a few copies at a time and allow others to enter the electronic queue.

❖ Program large print jobs to run either at night or on the weekend.

❖ Printing during work hours should be reserved for high priority items.

❖ Never turn off the printer unless you have been specifically asked to do so. It can stop the work flow of the entire office.

❖ Learn how to restock paper in the printer.

❖ Never use office equipment for personal use.

Also, avoid loading special papers (glossy, transparency) in a printer. It may damage or jam the unit. Use the copy machine for such work. Also, if you have both a color printer and a black and white, use the equipment for its intended use. Never print a black and white document on a full-color printer.

### *What steps can I take to make sure others have equal use of the printing equipment?*

*L*earn as much as possible about the technical aspects of computer printing. Understand that complicated graphics are

*NEVER TURN OFF THE PRINTER UNLESS YOU HAVE BEEN SPECIFICALLY ASKED TO DO SO.*

*MANNERS
ARE
EQUALLY AS
IMPORTANT AS
MACHINES.*

going to take much longer to print, so avoid busy times for such work.

Practice patience! Don't continue to send duplicate print orders if your job is not ready. There may be a long queue and you'll be wasting paper when the printer finally responds.

If the printer does not accept your file, don't automatically resend. Learn the reason for the rejection.

*W*hen using faxes, copiers and printers, always remember that manners are equally as important as machines.

# CHAPTER SIX

# DIGITAL COURTESIES
# IN PUBLIC PLACES

In a Florida dental office, a patient motioned for Dr. Leroy McCloud to wait. For the next fifteen minutes the man, seated in the dental chair, chatted on his cell phone.

Finally, Dr. McCloud asked the man to leave the office. "I don't have tolerance for that," said the dentist.

Dave Gussow, discussing the problem in the *St. Petersburg Times* (FL), cited these examples of cell phone abuse:

❖ The Parliament in India installed jamming devices to stop members from taking calls in the middle of debates.

❖ Three people have been jailed in Peoria, IL, because their cell phones rang in courtrooms.

*BE CAREFUL! A RINGING CELL PHONE CAN SEND YOU TO JAIL!*

❖ President George W. Bush had to admonish an aide after a ringing cell phone interrupted a meeting with Israeli Prime Minister Ariel Sharon.

Since electronic devices have permeated society, we need to be aware of how we use them in offices, restaurants, on public transportation and at social gatherings.

# AIRLINE ETIQUETTE

Frequent flyers are often surprised to learn that the rules regarding use of personal electronic devices vary greatly between airlines. Some carriers allow passengers to work on their laptops from the moment they leave the gate, while others make you wait until the plane has reached an altitude of 10,000 feet.

Not all electronic devices are restricted. Airlines have no problem with hearing aids and pacemakers. Most airlines, however, restrict use of some devices during takeoff and landing, including: shavers, portable CD and tape players, laptops and printers, calculators, handheld computer games, video players and portable DVDs.

Items which are totally banned in flight include: remote-controlled toys, televisions, cell phones, AM/FM radio

*THE MOST DIS-TINGUISHED HALLMARK OF THE AMERICAN SOCIETY IS AND ALWAYS HAS BEEN CHANGE.*

*– ERIC SEVAREID*

transmitters or receivers.

Don't ignore the rules when flying. In some countries, people have actually received jail sentences for refusing to obey electronic flight regulations.

### *Why can't I use my cell phone on an airplane?*

*S*ome people wonder, "If I can't use my wireless phone in flight, why do planes provide mobile phones for a fee?" The answer is that the air phones operate on an assigned air-ground frequency that does not interfere with the navigational equipment of the aircraft.

To be on the safe side, turn off *all* electronic devices until you are specifically told you may use them. The moment the aircraft door is closed, turn off your cell phone.

### *What are the rules of in-flight courtesy regarding laptop computers?*

*A*lthough it may be necessary at times, a cross-country flight is not an ideal atmosphere to work on your computer. And it's certainly

*BE ON THE SAFE SIDE. TURN OFF ALL ELECTRONIC DEVICES IN FLIGHT.*

not pleasant when the person in front of you suddenly reclines the back of his seat and pushes your laptop into your stomach.

If you must use your laptop, follow these rules:

*TURN OFF THE VOLUME. THOSE NOISES MAY IMPRESS YOUR FRIENDS, BUT NOT YOUR SEATMATE.*

❖ Request a window seat. You'll find a little more space and you can angle the screen for maximum privacy.

❖ Turn off the volume. Those noises may impress your friends, but not your seatmate.

❖ Never pretend the aircraft is your office. Just because the passenger in the center seat is not using his pull-down tray doesn't mean you can seize it to spread out your work.

❖ Don't pull out your laptop until the pilot announces that it is okay to use electronic devices. It's true that computers can interfere with the positioning and communication devices of aircraft.

Here is a word of advice for passengers: Avoid the temptation to read the screen of your neighbor's laptop. Respect his or her privacy.

### What rules should I follow if I use a portable DVD player on a flight?

*S*ome passengers would rather bring their own portable DVD player than watch the in-flight movie. If that is your preference:

❖ Always use audio headsets. Don't force your neighbors to listen to something they are not watching.
❖ Position the screen for "you-only" viewing. As with using laptops, try to secure a window seat.
❖ Keep quiet! Laughing out loud and making comments to your seatmate is unacceptable.

# RESTAURANTS AND ELECTRONICS

*A* growing number of restaurants are placing signs at the entrance podium that read: "Cell phones may not be used in the dining room. If you need to make or receive calls, please use our pay phone area."

Similar rules should also apply to the use of laptops and hand-held computer devices. The purpose of visiting a restaurant is to enjoy a meal and to engage in polite conversation. Anything that disturbs fellow diners – even those at your

*ANYTHING THAT DISTURBS FELLOW DINERS – EVEN AT YOUR TABLE – SHOULD BE AVOIDED.*

table – should be avoided.

While dining, either turn your cell phone off, or set on the "vibration" mode. If you are expecting an important call, excuse yourself and keep the conversation short. You show respect to your guests when you give them your undivided attention.

There are additional rules for cell phone etiquette in Chapter One.

*You Show Respect to Your Guests when You Give them Your Undivided Attention.*

## PUBLIC PHONE COURTESIES

*W*aiting in line for someone to finish a conversation on a pay phone or courtesy phone (such as in a hotel lobby) can be exasperating – especially if you need to make an urgent call. When you are calling from a public phone, follow these rules:

❖ Keep your conversations short; no more than two minutes.
❖ If you are using coins to place a long distance call, make sure you have extra change handy.
❖ Avoid placing multiple calls. This is not your office.
❖ Except for an absolute emergency, never ask someone to call you at the number of the pay phone.

Finally, keep your voice volume low. Those nearby don't need to hear your end of the conversation.

# ATM ETIQUETTE

It's more than annoying to approach an automatic teller machine and have someone standing a few inches behind you. Don't consider it rude to say, "Excuse me, may I have some privacy?"

Follow these rules:

- ❖ Stand close to the machine so that the person behind you cannot see the code you punch in, or the video monitor.
- ❖ If you have a large number of transactions to make, return later when the ATM is not busy.
- ❖ When you have finished, make certain you take your card and receipt. Don't be tempted to throw the receipt into the trash container. File or dispose of it properly at home.
- ❖ Make certain the video monitor has returned to the "home" screen before you leave.

Also, when standing in line, always create a two to three

*DON'T CONSIDER IT RUDE TO SAY, "EXCUSE ME, MAY I HAVE SOME PRIVACY?"*

foot buffer zone between you and the person using the machine.

# CREDIT CARD COURTESIES

*A*t a major department store, the line at the cashier's desk grew quite long when a man's credit card purchase was electronically disapproved. "That's impossible," said the customer. "I just used the card this morning. Let me speak to the manager." Meanwhile, those standing in line grew very restless.

Here are five rules you should follow when using credit cards.

1. If the customer behind you is paying by cash, allow that person to go first.
2. Have your card ready *before* the bill is presented. Don't fumble through your wallet or purse.
3. Know your credit limit and account balance at all times so that your purchase will be approved.
4. If, for any reason, there is a delay in processing, offer to step aside and allow other customers to make their purchases.
5. Always take your receipt with you and compare it

*If, for any reason, there is a delay in processing, offer to step aside and allow other customers to make their purchases.*

with your billing statement – whether from a restaurant or a retail store.

6. *Never* throw a receipt that includes your credit card number into a public trash container.

# MICROPHONE MANNERS

*Y*ou may have a great speaking voice and a polished stage presence, but if you don't know how to use a microphone properly, your ability to communicate during a presentation is greatly diminished.

### *What are the rules for using clip-on or lavalier microphones?*

*D*epending on the venue, you may be asked to use a microphone attached to your clothing. If so, follow these guidelines:

❖ Do not attach a clip-on microphone near a piece of jewelry.

❖ To pick up your voice properly, the microphone should be attached rather high on your lapel, tie or blouse.

❖ Always test the microphone prior to the event.

*DO NOT ATTACH A CLIP-ON MICROPHONE NEAR A PIECE OF JEWELRY.*

### What is considered proper use of wireless and stationary mikes?

A microphone, whether wireless or stationary, should be kept at a distance of approximately eight to ten inches from your mouth.

Avoid the tendency to place the microphone directly in front of your mouth. In most cases, the audio signal will be distorted. The ideal location is a few inches below and forward of your chin. That also makes it possible for your audience to see your complete face. Remember, communication is enhanced when people can also read your lips. That's impossible if they are covered by a microphone.

Many professional speakers prefer a hand-held wireless microphone since they can pull it away from their mouth (or bring it closer) for emphasis and volume control.

Stationary microphones should not be handled unnecessarily since they can result in unwanted noise.

*A MICROPHONE SHOULD BE KEPT AT A DISTANCE OF APPROXIMATELY EIGHT TO TEN INCHES FROM YOUR MOUTH.*

# MUSIC ETIQUETTE

Digital downloading, satellite signals and CDs have revolutionized the way we obtain and enjoy music. Never has so much entertainment been available to so many. However, there are standards of personal courtesy in the use of music which need to be obeyed.

### *Is it bad manners to put on a stereo headset and listen to a CD when others are present?*

There is a time for social interaction, and a time for private, personal enjoyment. In the presence of others, it is impolite to isolate yourself by listening to music. The exception is when a group decides they will *all* put on their headphones for a specified amount of time.

If the need to listen to your favorite music is of great importance, politely excuse yourself from the room and find a place to be alone.

### *What should be the response to an individual who loudly plays a boombox or blasts music from a car speaker system?*

Any person who invades the space of someone else is acting rude and discourteous. In most cases, loud music in public places is an adolescent cry for attention.

Many communities have regulations on excessive noise in public places. It should be our task to teach everyone how to treat others with honor, decency and respect – and that may include reducing the decibel level of music.

*ANY PERSON WHO INVADES THE SPACE OF SOMEONE ELSE IS ACTING RUDE AND DISCOURTEOUS.*

# VIDEO AND DIGITAL CAMERA COURTESIES

*F*ar too often the user of a hand-held camera becomes the center of attention – even more than the person being honored or the event being taped. Here are three important courtesies to remember:

*ALWAYS ASK PERMISSION OF THE HOST OR GUESTS BEFORE TAPING A PRIVATE EVENT.*

1. Always ask permission of the host or guests be fore taping a private event.
2. Keep a low profile and learn to be unobtrusive. That may require placing your camera on a tripod at a distance and using the zoom feature.
3. Don't feel you must capture every moment of the occasion. Anticipate the highlights and limit your photo time.

Whether at home or in public, when you truly respect and honor others, good manners will naturally follow.

# Chapter Seven

# Parents' Guide to Electronic Etiquette

In the life of a child, a world filled with digital gadgets, wireless phones and the Internet is as normal as breathing. For parents, however, this technology-driven culture has required a great amount of personal adjustment.

## Empowering Parents

It is the responsibility of parents or care givers to make sure their children have the knowledge and understanding of electronic etiquette.

Teach them that the use of electronic media by children is a privilege, not a right.

Permission is given to use such devices when children agree to act in a responsible, ethical and considerate manner.

*The use of electronic media by children is a privilege, not a right.*

*HAVE A WORKING KNOWLEDGE OF YOUR HOME COMPUTER BEFORE ALLOWING YOUR CHILD TO HAVE ACCESS.*

While the principles of good manners never change, they must be specifically applied to electronic devices.

Why is it important to set boundaries for your children at an early age? The principles you establish are building blocks that will help shape their character and attitude concerning electronic devices. These courtesies teach young people how to treat family, friends and others with respect.

Here are parent-child guidelines regarding use of computers, phones, music and digital games.

# COMPUTER ISSUES

The explosion in communications technology – including e-mail and the Internet – has made it possible for children to gain new knowledge and enjoy varied cultural experiences. Plus computer knowledge is considered *essential* in the preparation for college and career.

### As a parent, what are my responsibilities regarding a child's use of the computer?

Here are seven rules to follow:

1. Have a working knowledge of your home computer before allowing your child to have access.
2. If you aren't computer literate, it may mean taking a short course offered by a computer retail store or a

local college.

3. Keep the lines of communication open. Discuss the potential online dangers and instruct your child concerning the responsible use of the computer and online resources.

4. The computer should never be in a child's bedroom, but rather in a highly visible area of the home with the monitor facing the center of the room where parents can view it. Children should not be isolated from interaction with other family members.

5. Visit your child's school and local library and discuss current safeguards they are using to protect children.

6. Have a discussion with the parents of your child's friends so there is common agreement regarding computer use.

7. Before allowing your child access to a computer learn how to install and set age-appropriate security features.

**How effective are filters and "blocking" software in keeping harmful material from being accessed?**

*A* wide range of parental control technologies are available that can block content including violence, profanity, hate speech, pornography, drug culture, sex education, gambling and more. Some even completely prohibit access to newsgroups and chat sites.

*EVERY PARENT MUST BE THE GATEKEEPER OF THE MESSAGES BEING SENT TO A CHILD.*

*– DONNA DILLEY, COTILLION DIRECTOR, ROANOKE, VA*

Talk with your Internet service provider concerning blocking software and other available controls. They can direct you to programs that have special features, including limiting computer time, keeping a log of all activity, and those that enable parents to decide which applications are to be allowed.

Popular blocking programs include CYBERsitter, Net Nanny and CyberPatrol. Simply type the words "Internet filters" in any search engine and you'll find a wealth of knowledge.

A word of caution. Many parents make the assumption that electronic filters will keep all unwanted material out of their home. You can never be 100 percent certain. Remember, there is no software that can substitute for the concern and guidance of parents.

*TAKE A PRO-ACTIVE APPROACH TO YOUR CHILD'S USE OF THE COMPUTER.*

Take a pro-active approach to your child's use of the computer. You do this by setting appropriate boundaries and adding proper filters and blocks.

Of course, the best protection is for parents to "be there."

**What boundaries and rules of etiquette should be set so that my children will have a positive computer experience?**

*W*e cannot over-emphasize that appropriate guidelines are essential to the healthy development of a child. Boundaries send a message to children that they are loved – and that their parents care what happens to them. It also helps to build self-confidence because they know what is expected of them.

Follow these guidelines:

- ❖ Children should be taught to *always* ask their parents, "May I use the computer?"
- ❖ Set specific times your child may, or may not, use the computer.
- ❖ Children should never attempt to bypass home computer security devices.
- ❖ Passwords must not be shared outside of the immediate family.
- ❖ Explain to your child that downloading pirated music or unauthorized software is illegal and dishonest.
- ❖ Discuss computer ethics with your child. For example: No "hacking" into other sites or experimenting with computer viruses.

## GUIDELINES FOR PARENTS

**As a parent, how can I help safeguard my child's Internet experience?**

*O*n far too many homes, the computer has become an

*MAN IS STILL THE MOST EXTRA-ORDINARY COMPUTER OF ALL.*

*– JOHN F. KENNEDY*

"electronic babysitter" and children spend hours at the keyboard – unsupervised. Don't allow that to happen.

Start with a family discussion of the topic and be specific concerning what you consider off-limits regarding Internet use in your home. Follow these guidelines:

*YOUNG CHILDREN SHOULD NOT BE ALLOWED TO SURF THE INTERNET ALONE – LET IT BECOME A FAMILY ACTIVITY.*

❖ If you are not a personal Internet user, learn how to use it. For example, you can personally view the entire history of every site that has been accessed.

❖ Young children should not be allowed to surf the Internet alone – let it become an all-family activity.

❖ Set limits on the amount of time your child spends with the computer. (We recommend a maximum of one hour per day.) Parental software is available that includes time limit tools.

NOTE: If your child has access to an office computer (in or outside your home) which does not have Internet filters or security devices, make certain you monitor it carefully.

Unfortunately, young people are often vulnerable to exploitation because of the nature of the Internet. It is important for parents to know how to protect their families while at the same time benefitting from this new technology.

## What guidelines should parents establish for children who use Instant Messaging or e-mail?

Teach your child that there is a real person at the other end of the message. Always treat that individual with the utmost respect.

Emphasize the fact that e-mail messages are not private. Explain that they are the equivalent of an electronic post card, and are easily accessible by others.

Time limits should be placed on communicating with friends via Instant Messaging. We recommend a maximum of fifteen minutes per session. Also, to respect the private times of others, IM should be used only between the hours of 9:00 A.M. and 9:00 P.M.

Never allow your child to enter chat rooms of unknown individuals. Limit e-mail conversations to a "buddy list" he or she is acquainted with. Personally approve the list your child uses with Instant Messaging. Make sure his or her "screen name" is appropriate, and review the profiles of your own child and his or her "buddies." Be sure there is no improper or offensive language.

Know your child's passwords and, for safety reasons, check his or her e-mail and "buddy list" regularly.

Remember, you are not simply setting rules, but teaching your children the importance of respecting themselves and their friends.

*Teach Your Child That There Is A Real Person At The Other End Of The Message.*

### *What should I do if my child has been solicited online?*

*Y*ou should report any unusual activity coming into your home – the sending of child pornography, attempts to lure a child, posts concerning bomb making or terrorism, or any physical threat. This is prohibited by Federal law.

Immediately contact either your Internet service provider, local law enforcement agency, the FBI or the National Center for Missing and Exploited Children (1-800-843-5678).

In such cases, turn off the computer to preserve evidence. Let a law enforcement officer analyze the data on your computer.

## A COVENANT FOR KIDS

*Y*ou should ask your child to make the following agreement with you:

> ❖ "I will always ask permission before using the computer."
>
> ❖ "I will always tell my parents if I see something online that I don't understand."
>
> ❖ "I will always ask permission before using my full name or sharing personal information online."
>
> ❖ "I will never give out a credit card number or a password online."

*I WILL ALWAYS ASK PERMISSION BEFORE USING MY FULL NAME OR SHARING PERSONAL INFORMATION ONLINE.*

- ❖ "I will not respond to any message that makes me feel uncomfortable."
- ❖ "I will never phone or accept a phone call from someone who has contacted me online."
- ❖ "I will always tell my parents if someone online asks to meet with me."
- ❖ "I will not give out personal information about my friends."

Instruct your child never to give a home address, phone number, what school he or she attends – or any data which would allow someone to be able to locate your child.

# ON THE PHONE

*T*eaching phone etiquette should begin at age three and continue through the formative years. We recommend purchasing a "play phone" to teach a young child correct phone manners. If early instruction is avoided, the child will develop phone habits that are difficult to break.

Start by having practice sessions with your children to teach them to speak clearly and distinctly when on the phone. Children should be taught to know why they are calling and to stick to the subject.

A child should not answer the phone until he or she is old enough to clearly write a message for you (usually around the

*I will never phone or accept a phone call from someone who has contacted me online.*

age of six). The only exception is if you are in the room and are teaching the child to answer the phone.

Show your child how to properly dial 911. Explain the difference between a real emergency (such as a fire or someone breaking into the home) and a non-emergency.

In Richmond, Virginia, a four-year-old was at home on Friday night with the baby sitter. Suddenly, the cat slipped out of the door and ran down the street. The girl and the sitter instantly ran after the cat, but a stray dog chased the girl's pet up a tree. Immediately, the little girl ran inside and dialed 911, shouting, "There is an emergency. Something terrible has happened. Please come quick!"

The police arrived about the same time the cat came home. Later, the girl's parents had a chance to discuss when – and when *not* – to dial 911.

### Should children have their own telephones?

*A*void placing a phone in your child's room. Children should not have personal phones in their rooms until they are of an age to accept the responsibility to pay for them. Even if a young person has his or her own phone and pays for it with an allowance or personal funds, the child must abide by time limits and other rules of phone use.

Long telephone conversations with friends can destroy family interaction and lower school grades.

*CHILDREN SHOULD NOT HAVE PERSONAL PHONES IN THEIR ROOMS UNTIL THEY ARE OF AN AGE TO ACCEPT THE RESPONSIBILITY TO PAY FOR THEM.*

Cell phones should only be given to children for reasons of safety – not for social calls. We recommend that if a child has a wireless phone, it should be "on loan" and for the purpose of calling home. Children should not be allowed to give the number to friends.

### *Specifically, what guidelines should I give my child concerning phone use?*

*H*ere are ten practical rules:

1. Never enter into phone conversations with someone you don't know.
2. If you are home alone, for safety reasons do not tell the caller, "My parents are not home." Instead, say, "He (or she) is not available right now. May I take a message?"
3. Show your child how to properly use "Call Waiting." It could be an emergency or an extremely important call.
4. Never place an order on the phone using a credit card without permission.
5. Do not place a call from someone else's phone without your host's permission.
6. Do not answer the phone of another person unless you are asked to do so.
7. If you have been given a cell phone or beeper so

*Do Not Place a Call From Someone Else's Phone Without Your Host's Permission.*

that your parents can reach you, be polite, respectful and responsible by turning down the ring volume (or use vibration mode) in public places. Make sure the battery is fully charged.

8. A cell phone call or beeper message from a parent must be returned within seven minutes.

9. Do not take a cordless phone into the bathroom – for obvious reasons.

10. Return the cordless phone to its proper location after every call.

After more than a quarter-century of teaching etiquette to young people, the following three rules are considered the most important regarding telephone manners for children:

1. Do not make or receive calls before 9:00 A.M. or after 9:00 P.M. (or during meal times).

2. Calls should be limited to no longer than twelve to fifteen minutes, and should be for a specific purpose. For example: to discuss a school assignment.

3. Calls between children are not "just to talk."

Also, teach your child how to place and receive calls, and how to take and leave messages. These are discussed in Chapter Two.

Adults should set the example for their children that the telephone is not for idle chatter or hours of gossip. While we may not think children are listening, they really are – and they

*Adults Should Set The Example For Their Children That The Telephone Is Not For Idle Chatter Or Hours Of Gossip.*

will imitate our example. Young people are forming lasting attitudes and patterns for their own behavior. Make sure your conversations are uplifting and positive.

Being respectful of others is a lifelong step-by-step process that must start early. Always explain *why* a rule of etiquette is being established and enforced in your home.

# ELECTRONIC GAMES

*W*ith the excuse that they are "really great for hand-eye coordination," parents have allowed video gaming systems to become electronic baby-sitters. Unfortunately, excessive use of such games can lead to anti-social behavior. A child is also at risk of being exposed to dangers through the content of the games themselves.

Know exactly what your child is playing with. Many parents are shocked to discover that extreme violence and sexual content are not limited to "R" rated motion pictures. Their children may be exposed to the same images on a two-inch screen.

The purchase of a game should be made by the parent, not the child. You should personally examine the content of an electronic game before buying it.

Parents must establish these rules:

❖ It is rude to ignore the presence of family and friends while engrossed in a particular game.

*Always Explain Why a Rule of Etiquette Is Being Established in Your Home.*

*THE FAMILY*
*TELEVISION*
*SET IS NOT*
*TO BE*
*DOMINATED*
*BY A CHILD*
*WHO USES IT*
*FOR A GAME*
*CENTER.*

❖ When guests arrive, children should stop what they are playing and engage in polite conversation.

❖ Keep the audio volume of an electronic game at the lowest possible level.

❖ The family television set is not to be dominated by a child who uses it for a game center.

❖ On long journeys by car, set limits on the amount of time a child may use a portable electronic game. Family interaction must remain primary.

❖ During short visits with relatives or friends, there will be no playing of electronic games. Instead, children should be involved in conversation.

Don't allow the tail to wag the dog. Game-playing should be limited to short periods of time and be seen as entertainment – not something that dominates the life of a child.

# MUSIC AND YOUR CHILD

A father complained, "I never get to talk with my thirteen-year-old daughter anymore. From the time I get home from work until bedtime, she has those headsets on – listening to who knows what!"

In many homes – by default – the rules have been set by children rather than parents. Perhaps it is time for the family to have a lengthy conversation on the topic of music in the home. As a parent it is your responsibility to establish clear guidelines for use of portable CDs and stereo systems.

- ❖ Set the times your children may listen to music.
- ❖ Meal times should be for family conversation.
- ❖ Loud music played on stereos and "boomboxes" should not become the atmosphere of the home.

In addition, parents should listen to the lyrics of the CDs their children bring into the home. Offensive language or harmful messages should not be allowed in any form.

The National League of Junior Cotillions screens all music used in its hundreds of chapters nationwide. We believe that positive music can help reinforce the manners we all need to possess.

### How can I teach my child about the potential hearing loss that may result from listening to loud music?

*P*rior to the teenage years, in the presence of your family doctor, have a conversation with your child regarding possible permanent damage that can result from excessive noise. It's a serious issue.

Here are the facts. When sustained decibel levels exceed 85 for even thirty minutes, hearing deterioration can occur. Amplified rock music is usually between 110 and 130 decibels.

We have seen young people "bouncing" and even singing out loud while listening to their headsets in public places.

*MEAL TIMES SHOULD BE FOR FAMILY CONVERSATION.*

Obviously, the music was too loud.

Teach your child to take these precautions:

❖ At concerts, always wear earplugs. You'll still hear quite well.
❖ Never stand near a concert loud speaker.
❖ When listening to your personal stereo (either in a room or with earphones) avoid high volumes.

Understand that constant "pounding" music, if listened to for prolonged periods, can result in significant hearing loss.

Teach your child to be aware of warning signs such as dull hearing or ringing in the ear. Even if the symptoms last for only a short time, they are a signal that hearing damage may have taken place. And remember, the risk of such damage increases with lengthy exposure and greater volume.

James Strachan, the executive director of the Royal National Institute for Deaf People in Great Britain, says, "The evidence is clear – loud music can damage your hearing and . . . more young people than ever are putting themselves at risk."

### When my child is old enough to drive, what rules regarding music in the car should be established?

*A*s a citizen, your teenager must act responsibly – and that should include a parental decision that prohibits blaring music from any automobile in the family.

*CONSTANT "POUNDING" MUSIC, IF LISTENED TO FOR PROLONGED PERIODS, CAN RESULT IN SIGNIFICANT HEARING LOSS.*

~

The issue involves more than respect for others. Many teens are killed on highways every year because their music drowns out the sound of an emergency vehicle siren or the honking of a horn.

Audio headsets should never be worn while driving. And the music volume of the radio must be low enough so that it won't interfere with a normal conversation.

If your child disobeys the rules you have established, don't hesitate to take away his or her driving privileges. If not, your child may face more serious consequences. For example, in Lakeland, Florida, playing loud music from cars is a criminal violation with up to a $1,000 fine and one year in jail. First time offenders are sentenced to "Music Court."

Music brings personal enjoyment, yet it should also reflect consideration for others.

*WHILE MUSIC BRINGS PERSONAL ENJOYMENT, IT SHOULD ALSO REFLECT CONSIDER-ATION FOR OTHERS.*

~

*W*hile computers, cell phones, DVDs and digital devices have drastically changed our world, they did not arrive with built-in manners or courtesies. Those must be applied by the users – you and me.

It is our desire that the rules, guidelines and principles found in *THE OFFICIAL BOOK OF ELECTRONIC ETIQUETTE* will be demonstrated as you treat others with honor, dignity and respect.

# INDEX

# About the National League of Cotillions™

The National League of Cotillions is the nation's only organization that trains and licenses directors to establish local cotillion programs. The first chapter was established in North Carolina in 1978 and the national expansion of the program began in 1989.

Today, thousands of students are being taught etiquette, social dance and character education in hundreds of cotillion programs presented by chapters in over 30 states. The programs include:

> PRE-COTILLION – pre kindergarten through fourth grade.
> JUNIOR COTILLION – fifth through eighth grades.
> HIGH SCHOOL COTILLION CLUB – ninth through twelfth grades.
> THE NATIONAL LEAGUE OF DEBUTANTE COTILLIONS™ – a post-high school presentation society for young women.
> INTERNATIONAL LEAGUE OF CORPORATE COTILLIONS™ – special programs for business, social groups, colleges and universities.
> PRE-ASSEMBLIES AND JUNIOR ASSEMBLIES – corporate sponsored scholarship programs for the economically deprived.

To fulfill its mission of making social and character education available in every community, the organization trains and licenses qualified Directors who are given an exclusive territory in which to present the program – either on a full time or part-time basis.

If you are interested in contacting a local chapter in your area, or obtaining information on becoming a Director, visit the official website: www.nljc.com.

THE NATIONAL LEAGUE OF COTILLIONS
P.O. Box 240384
Charlotte, NC 28224
Phone: 1-800-633-7947
Fax: 1-704-846-3232
E-mail: cotillions@nljc.com.
Internet: www.nljc.com